NEUROSURGEON IN WAR AND PEACE

AMEEN ABBAS AMEEN

Ordering Information:

BookTrail Agency
8838 Sleepy Hollow Rd.
Kansas City, MO 64114

Printed in the United States of America

If I had the knowledge of Al Ghaib (The Unseen), I should have
secured an abundance of wealth and no evil would have touched me.
—Surah al-Aaraf 188, the Holy Koran

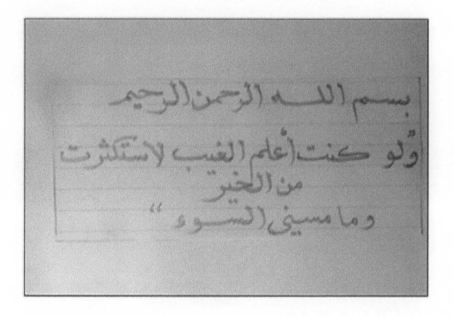

TABLE OF CONTENTS

PREFACE

AFTER HAVING IGNORED MY WIFE'S many years' encouragement to write a book about my rare and special experience in managing the wounded victims of the three wars in Iraq, followed by peaceful neurosurgery service in four countries, it was Robin Illingworth's inspirational comment describing the idea as "splendid" that prompted me at last to write this book.

Robin was my consultant (with Martin Rice Edwards) when I was a registrar at the Central Middlesex Hospital in London (1977–1980). I kept contacting him as a teacher and treasured friend since I left the UK and returned to Iraq in 1980.

His hard work culminated in moving the neurosurgical unit from the Central Middlesex Hospital to Charing Cross Hospital, London, a few years after I left, where I also kept doing locum posts arranged by Robin, coming from Iraq nearly every year to do so.

My family and I survived the indiscriminate artillery shelling of the city of Basrah during the eight years of the Iraq–Iran war (1980–1988), followed by the airplane bombardments of Iraq and the burning of my house from bombing by Saddam's forces in the aftermath of the 1990 war to crush the resistance. Miraculously, we escaped death countless number of times. When I wrote to Robin from Iraq during this period, he agreed that I do probably have nine lives.

Following his two visits to Basrah during the war, Robin Illingworth described my experience in his reference to the Joint Committee of Higher Surgical Training at the Royal College of surgeons (JCHST) in London as: "Ameen probably has the largest experience of anyone in the world with missile injuries of the brain."

The Holy Quran's verse with which this text begins reminds me of the continuous educational process and thorough discussion nearly all UK neurosurgeons (and probably all other specialists) do in their daily morning meetings, as well as the less frequent monthly mortality and morbidity meetings to discuss and plan further management of patients admitted the day before. These meetings are meant to revise the decision made the day before and acknowledge and learn from any mistakes made in order to avoid repeating them. Alas, this can rarely be achieved because although we continuously learn lessons from these meetings, the truth remains that mistakes and complications happen all the time despite the recurrent lessons.

For all of the stated reasons, I became tempted to write this book for general readers, hoping that they will enjoy it as a story of my life with nearly forty-three years' experience in neurosurgery, including the eight years of treating war victims of the Iran–Iraq war followed by my neurosurgery work in three other countries: Jordan, Qatar, and the UK. I have also included briefly my experience in reporting on the challenging clinical negligence claims during my twenty-two years of medico legal report writing.

To share my experience with other neurosurgeons, I tried my best to highlight the mistakes I made and the hard lessons I learnt, as well as report some interesting teaching cases I dealt with.

I am indebted for Suhaila (my wife; without her, I wouldn't have published this book), my son Ahmad, my daughters Sally, Rasha, Ruba, and Robin Illingworth for their great support and encouragement to write this book.

I hope this book will be of interest to the general reader as well as convey useful lessons and messages to other colleagues, junior doctors in training, and medical students, including the many I have trained and taught since 1980.

CHAPTER 1

The Beginning of My Career in Medicine

MY FAMILY DIDN'T HAVE A medical background; my father was a teacher, and my mother was a housewife. During my primary and secondary schooling, I had always been one of the top two or three students in my class. When I qualified from my secondary school in Kadhimiya, Baghdad, in 1964, I was ranked tenth among those who qualified in Iraq (population near 8.2 million at the time), with an average mark of 91 out of 100 in all subjects. I was easily accepted into Baghdad Medical College. Medicine has always been the favourite career to choose in Iraq—and probably everywhere else.

Education in Iraq has always been free, including university study, because the country is one of the most oil-rich in the world, holding the fifth largest proven crude oil reserves. All qualified postgraduate candidates sent on scholarship abroad are paid a monthly stipend by the government during their years of study to cover living expenses as well as university and examination fees.

I qualified from Baghdad University Medical College in 1970 with the highest distinction grade of "very good" in the university system. I then spent the next five years completing the resident internship programme, military service in Baghdad, and two years as a resident surgical registrar in Basra, during which I passed the primary FRCS exam held yearly by the Royal College of Surgeons of England in Baghdad.

The first medical school in Iraq was the Iraqi Royal Medical College, now called Baghdad College of Medicine, founded in 1927 by a group of Iraqi doctors who graduated from international medical schools.

THE BRITISH INFLUENCE

Harry Sanderson, a British physician, was the first dean of the college. He established the first medical curriculum in coordination with the Royal College of Surgeons of Edinburgh and set a strategic plan for medical education in Iraq. In subsequent years, the Royal Medical College in Baghdad developed and presented itself as one of the best medical schools in the Arab world in terms of academic teaching and research.

Born in Caistor, Lincolnshire, Sanderson graduated from the Faculty of Medicine, University of Edinburgh, in 1914. He participated in World War I as an army doctor. He was posted to Iraq in 1918 and was seconded to the British administration as Deputy Director of Civil Medical Services. In 1919 and 1920, he worked as a surgeon in Hillah and Baghdad, and later was in charge of various hospitals in Baghdad. In 1927, he helped to establish a new medical school in Baghdad, which became the Royal Medical College when the King of Iraq opened its new building in 1930. From 1923, Sanderson was personal physician to Iraq's kings. He served as Dean of the Medical College from 1927 until 1934, and again from 1941 until 1946, when he retired and returned to live in Sussex, England.

Sanderson played a significant role in the development of health and medical education in modern Iraq, following the country's establishment by the British in 1920. He was personal physician to the royal family of Iraq and a confidant to King Faisal I and then to the Prince Regent, and he played an important role in the politics of that period.

The educational system in Iraq has always been influenced by the British. I learned English language first as a compulsory subject in the primary school at the age of eleven years; it was the only foreign language taught in all government schools.

All subjects taught in Iraq medical schools were in English, apart from Forensic Medicine. We nearly always had British lecturers and examiners, who also come to assess difficult selected patients and high- ranked officers in the government. Complicated medical or surgical patients preferred to be treated in Britain if they could afford it.

From the mid-seventies, the Royal colleges of surgeons and physicians in the UK have established examination centres for the part 1 exam of the fellowship and membership of these colleges preceded by two to three months educational course.

The majority of the teaching staff in Iraq medical colleges have their membership or fellowships from the UK, and hence the ambitions from the days of being medical student is to complete our postgraduate training in Britain.

IRAQ AND BRITAIN: A 103-YEAR HISTORY

The Fall of Baghdad occurred on 11 March 1917 during the Mesopotamia campaign fought between the forces of the British Indian Army and the Ottoman Turkish Empire in the First World War. Iraq passed from the falling Ottoman Empire into British control. The British established the Kingdom of Iraq in 1932.

The present state of Iraq was founded by Britain in 1920 on land of great historical antiquity known as Mesopotamia. The country lay between two rivers, the Tigris and Euphrates, and was the birthplace of the ancient civilisations of Sumer, Babylon, and Nineveh. The present capital of Iraq, Baghdad, lies near Babylon and was founded by the Arab Abbasid dynasty in the eighth century AD. This was the glittering city of *Arabian Nights* and of Harun al-Rashid, which in 1258 was destroyed by the invading Mongols and became a provincial backwater until it was conquered again—this time in 1534 by the Ottomans, who made it the chief city of the Province of Baghdad. Eventually, separate provinces of Mosul to the north and Basra to the south were created. These three provinces looked out in different directions. Mosul was a mountainous region largely inhabited by Kurds, and it looked north to neighbouring Turkish Anatolia. Baghdad looked across the deserts to Syria and east to Persia. Finally, Basra and the head of the Persian Gulf looked seaward as far as India.

In the nineteenth century, Europeans—largely the British—began to take an interest in exploring, surveying, spying, and trading in

Mesopotamia, as well as in navigating its rivers. By 1914, there was growing anxiety about the security of the Persian oil fields on the other side of the Gulf. These were the fields that supplied the Royal Navy.

The Ottoman Empire entered World War I on the side of Germany and immediately became an enemy of Britain and France. Allied operations attacked Ottoman holdings. The first Mesopotamia campaign invading Iraq from India failed. The second captured Baghdad in 1917.

THE BEGINNING OF IRAQ INSTABILITY

In the 14 July Revolution of 1958, the king of Iraq was deposed and the Republic of Iraq was declared, which I remember very well because I was eleven years old. Abd al-Karim Qasim was an Iraqi Army brigadier and nationalist who ascended into power when the Iraqi monarchy was overthrown during the 14 July Revolution. He ruled the country as the 24th Prime Minister until his downfall and execution during the 1963 Ramadan Revolution.

Qasim, (Wikipedia, the free encyclopedia) despite his military and arbitrary dictatorship, remained the most prominent symbol of Iraqi patriotism in the country's modern history: As a result of the coup he led on July 14, 1958, Iraq emerged from the policy of alliances, of which Baghdad was the most important capital. In his struggle with the Arab nationalists and the Baathists, he was establishing the Iraqi patriotism that is not affiliated with Nasserite Egypt.

While studying in the secondary school, I witnessed the Ba'ath Party coup d'état in 1963, which overthrow Abdul Karim Kasim, who I remember was very popular amongst most Iraqis. He ignored the pre-revolution plan with his fellow revolutionist army officers to set up an elected government after the success of the 1958 revolution against the monarchy of King Faisal II and stayed in power as the prime minister and general head of the army. I recall many attempts by his military colleagues, who set up the 1958 revolutions with him, to overthrow him, during which our education at the secondary school was interrupted for few days or even weeks. This always reminds me of the many other famous leaders in the world who start as freedom fighters only to stay in power for as long as they can until they are overthrown by another revolution or by the superpower (usually the American or the British) who often brought them to power in the first place; some examples are Gaddafi and most Arab revolutionary leaders.

My parents were very careful to keep me and my two brothers (now both consultants in the UK) away from being involved with any political activities in Iraq, mainly because of the dangers involved of being imprisoned, injured, or killed by the government or the opposing political parties, who communicate with each other by guns only. The dream of those involved in politics is the fulfilment of their ambition of becoming a minister or the head of a political party, with all the privileges and the popularity that comes with it.

The Baath Party was in turn toppled by another coup in the same year in 1963, though they managed to retake power in 1968. Saddam Hussein came to power in this coup and became vice president first and then the president in 1979. He ruled Iraq for the remainder of the century until he was overthrown from power by the American and the British following the invasion of Iraq in 2003.

AFTER MY GRADUATION FROM THE MEDICAL SCHOOL IN 1970

In the 1970s, Iraq was very prosperous and stable. Its relationship with Britain was excellent, and postgraduate training courses and exams for the FRCS and the MRCP in Baghdad were run yearly by the British Royal Colleges of Surgeons and Physicians.

The UK was still the first choice of Iraqi doctors intending to do a postgraduate specialisation in any medical subspecialty because Iraqis has big faith in anything British being trustworthy and honest.

Many of those who completed their training did not return to Iraq because of the worsening conditions from the three wars and the ensuing embargo which caused extreme economic hardship. Hence, they stayed in the UK, wanting a better and safer life for themselves and their children.

After my graduation from Baghdad Medical College in 1970, I spent the next five years completing one-year rotating resident internship programmes, spending equal time in medicine, surgery, obstetrics and gynaecology, and paediatrics. I then had one year of military service in Baghdad and two years as a resident surgical registrar in Basra, during which I passed the primary FRCS exam, held yearly by the Royal College of Surgeons of England in Baghdad. During those years, Saddam Hussein was fighting the Kurds in the north, who were struggling to gain their independence. There was the risk of being posted to the battlefield there during my military service, but because I was one of the top ten graduates in my class, I was appointed at Al Rasheed Military Hospital in Baghdad for a year, which was the main army referring medical centre for the whole of Iraq, with all medical and surgical specialities (except obstetrics and gynaecology) and modern medical and surgical equipment.

THE SCHOLARSHIP TO THE UK, 1975

In 1975, I was granted a two-year paid scholarship by Basra University to the UK to complete the requirement for the final FRCS exam, which I passed in 1977 from both Royal Colleges of England and Edinburgh.

When I left Basra for the UK in 1975, the only neurosurgical centre serving the whole country of Iraq was in Baghdad, almost 530 kilometres north of Basra. It is still functioning and overseen by the senior neurosurgeon in Iraq, Professor Saad al-Witry, who is recognised as the founder of neurosurgery in Iraq and who contributed significantly to neurosurgical service in Iraq over the last fifty-five years or so. Basra was deficient in many surgical specialities, including neurosurgery, and hence I was very encouraged by the Department of Surgery of Basra Medical College to choose neurosurgery or paediatric surgery as my career after I passed my FRCS exam in general surgery. All head injuries and simple neurosurgical cases in Basrah and surrounding provinces at that time were managed by the general surgeon on call, and other more complicated neurosurgical cases were referred to Baghdad Centre.

After passing the final FRCS exam in general surgery in 1977 from the Royal Colleges of both England and Edinburgh, I completed my one-year senior house officer post in St Albans City Hospital in general and orthopaedic surgery and started my post as resident neurosurgery registrar at Central Middlesex Hospital, London, in April 1977.

CHAPTER 2

My Registrar Post at the Central Middlesex Hospital, 1977–1980

MY WIFE AND I TREASURE those three years at Central Middlesex Hospital as the happiest days we spent in the UK, during which we had two children born at the hospital. We had two other daughters born later, during the wars in Basra.

I remember very well the day in 1977 when Robin Illingworth asked me to join him in the first ward round. He had told me that I was successful in my interview for the registrar job and described to me the field of neurosurgery as "fascinating".

At Central Middlesex Hospital, we were two registrars with twenty-four-hour on-call commitments one day and nine-to-five duties the next. The longest daily on-call commitment was for three months, when the other registrar and I attended the nine-to-five neurology and neurosurgery course at the National Hospital for Neurology and Neurosurgery, Queen Square, London, at two different periods, for which the hospital paid the fee.

During my post, I was provided with a two-bedroom flat on the grounds of Central Middlesex Hospital, which was very convenient during the frequent on-call commitments. Robin Illingworth and Martin Rice Edwards remained the only two consultants in the unit during this period, alternating the same twenty-four-hour on-call commitments as we did.

CT scans had just been introduced at Central Middlesex when I started, and at first, they were for elective cases only—hence we used to do cerebral angiography for emergency cases when required. I remember the first emergency burr hole operation I did for an unconscious patient with chronic subdural haematoma, diagnosed through cerebral angiography, who recovered fully the next morning, to my delight. A subdural hematoma (SDH) is a type of bleeding in which a collection of blood—usually associated with a traumatic brain injury—gathers between the inner layer of the dura mater and the arachnoid mater of the meninges surrounding the brain.

During those three years, I was exposed to nearly all elective and emergency neurosurgical cases and was allowed to operate on nearly all cases, except for aneurysm surgery and the difficult posterior cranial fossa cases, such as acoustic neuroma and trigeminal microvascular decompression. Robin took special interest in doing the latter, having visited the famous Peter Jannetta, who published his experience and technique in the *Journal of Neurosurgery.*

During my registrar post at the Central Middlesex Hospital, Robin designed a historical study on the effectiveness the drug Epsilon Aminocaproic acid in the prevention of recurrent bleeding in cases of subarachnoid haemorrhage. This drug is an antifibrinolytic agent used to prevent the lysis of the clot formed at the site of the bleeding and in other body parts as well.

In this study, I reviewed the case notes of two hundred consecutive patients with aneurysmal SAH, half of which were from before we used EACA, with one hundred later patients who had received it. We showed that the outcome in the two groups was similar; the reduction in bleeding rate in the treated group was balanced by an increase in ischaemia. We stopped using EACA and moved to an earlier operation, a change which was made more effective after the Nimodipine study (in which Robin participated) and which showed a 30 per cent improvement in outcome.

Our work was finally published in the *Journal of Neurology, Neurosurgery, and Psychiatry* in 1981, nearly a year after I returned to

Iraq. I was pleased to see my name coming up as the first author in this article, but deep in myself, I felt it should have been Robin's name first because he actually designed and wrote the paper. It was his generosity that led him to put my name first.

RETURNING TO IRAQ IN 1980

Because I stayed in the UK for three years, more than the two years the scholarship granted to me (with monthly salary to pass the FRCS exam) from Basrah University, I was forced to return to Iraq despite my unfinished neurosurgical training and without doing a senior registrar post (which Robin encouraged me very much to do when a vacant job came up in Southampton). The financial commitments I had made with the university before I left Iraq dictated that I had to pay 4,500 Iraqi dinar, which I received as a monthly salary in UK during the two years of my scholarship (the equivalent of nearly £140,000 at that time) to the university if I refused to go back at the end of my two-year scholarship in the UK. Interestingly, in today's value the 4,500 Iraqi dinar is equivalent to less than five pounds, given the extreme depreciation of the Iraqi currency after the three wars. I struggled with the authorities in Iraq, including the university and the Ministry of Higher Education, to postpone their demand to pay back this amount they paid me because I wanted to stay longer to complete my training for a much-needed speciality in Basra, but they refused, so I was forced to return to Basra in July 1980.

During my registrar post at the Central Middlesex Hospital, my wife found it difficult to look after our two children and complete her training for the MRCP paediatric exam, and hence she went back to Iraq with part I only to come back two years later to complete part II of the exam. I and my wife had to arrange our on-call commitments with the help of a baby minder. Robins commented at the time that my wife left her children to be looked after by the baby minder while she looked after other people's children.

I must say that the three years of neurosurgery training I had at the Central Middlesex Hospital with the one in two rotas (and sometimes one in one when one of us was absent for any reason), as well as the unlimited weekly working hours, was probably equivalent to the current six years of post-Calman training currently implemented prior to granting the certificate of completion of specialist training in the UK by the Royal College of Surgeons.

CHAPTER 3

My Neurosurgery Post in Basrah

I FIRST JOINED AS THE second neurosurgery consultant in Basrah in July 1980, nearly two months before the Iran–Iraq War erupted. The unit was still in its infancy and had started a few months before I arrived, with just one consultant (the late Mr Jaafar Al Nakeeb). It was the only unit in southern Iraq, the nearest being in Baghdad nearly 560 Kilometres north of Basrah. By the time I left Basrah in 1992, the unit had no working CT scan, which was imported early in 1980 but remained in closed boxes, uninstalled, in one of the hospital corridors. It was waiting during the war for the foreign engineers to install it because they refused to come to Basrah, fearing for their safety from the Iranian shelling.

THE LONGEST WAR IN THE TWENTIETH CENTURY

The Iraq–Iran War is considered to be the longest of wars in the twentieth century. It caused huge damage to both countries—even now, after nearly thirty-two years since the war ended, thousands of people are still suffering from the damage and lifelong disabilities they developed as a result of their horrific injuries (such as spinal injuries with paraplegia and injuries to the extremities with amputations).

Like most war injuries, it affected especially the youth and young adults in large numbers, aged eighteen to forty years old during the war. The long-lasting effects on their families were also dreadful.

The war (Wikipedia, the free encyclopedia) began on 22 September 1980, when Iraq invaded Iran and it ended on 20 August 1988, when Iran accepted the UN-brokered ceasefire. Iraq wanted to replace Iran as the dominant Persian Gulf state, and was worried the 1979 Iranian Revolution would lead Iraq's Shi'a majority to rebel against the Ba'athist government. The war also followed a long history of border disputes, and Iraq planned to annex the oil-rich Khuzestan Province and the east bank of the Shatt al-Arab.

Although Iraq hoped to take advantage of Iran's post-revolutionary chaos, it made limited progress and was quickly repelled; Iran regained virtually all lost territory by June 1982. For the next five years, Iran was on the offensive until Iraq took back the initiative in 1988, and whose major offensives lead to the final conclusion of the war. There were a number of proxy forces—most notably the People's Mujahedin of Iran siding with Iraq and the Iraqi Kurdish militias of the KDP and PUK siding with Iran. The United States, Britain, the Soviet Union, France, and most Arab countries provided political and logistic support for Iraq, while Iran was largely isolated.

At the end Saddam Hussein who initiated the war did not achieve what he wanted which was to reassert Iraq's <u>sovereignty</u> over both banks of the <u>Shatt al-'Arab</u>, a river formed by the <u>confluence</u> of the <u>Tigris and Euphrates rivers</u> that was historically the border between the two countries. Hence, he achieved nothing but the loss of lives and the damages he inflicted with Khomeini to both countries.

But under the leadership of <u>Ruhollah Khomeini</u>, who bore a strong personal animosity toward Saddam, Iran remained intransigent and continued the war in an effort to overthrow Saddam Hussein.

Iraq's defences solidified once its troops were defending their own soil, and the war settled down into a stalemate with a static, entrenched front running just inside and along Iraq's border. Iran repeatedly launched fruitless infantry attacks, using human assault waves composed partly of untrained and unarmed conscripts (often young boys snatched from the streets), which were repelled by the superior firepower and air power of the Iraqis. Both nations engaged in sporadic air and missile attacks against each other's cities and military and oil installations.

The number of casualties was enormous but equally uncertain. Estimates of total casualties range from 1,000,000 to twice that number. The number killed on both sides was perhaps 500,000, with Iran suffering the greatest losses. It is estimated that between 50,000 and 100,000 Kurds were killed by Iraqi forces during the series of campaigns code-named Anfāl (Arabic: "Spoils") that took place in 1988.

MY JOB IN BASRAH STARTED WITH THE WAR

As the war started in September 1980, nearly two months after my arrival to Basrah, everyone felt that my coming was very timely when a large number of head injury cases and much fewer spinal injuries from the nearby frontlines (Basrah city is nearly twenty miles away from the nearest Iranian border city of Khorramshahr) started occupying the whole neurosurgical unit. The eight floors of the teaching hospital I worked in were assigned for the war-injured victims, including Iraqi civilians from the Iranian shelling of the city of Basrah itself. Each of the main surgical specialties had its own ward and occupied (when possible) one floor: cardiothoracic, orthopaedic, general surgery, ophthalmology, and ENT. The orthopaedic speciality occupied most of the hospital beds because it included all cases with extensive soft tissue missile injuries to all body parts.

One floor accommodated the operating theatres, ITU, and recovery units only. Evacuation of those operated upon was done within twenty-four hours form all surgical specialities to Baghdad and other cities in the north. They moved in large numbers daily by train because the number of available beds in all Basrah hospitals was very often much less than those admitted daily.

We were two consultant neurosurgeons in Basrah serving the whole of southern Iraq; the next nearest unit was the main one in Baghdad, 330 miles north of Basrah. Because the war lasted for so many years, arrangement was made by the central government for most Iraqi surgeons to work for a week or two in Basra to make us feel that other Iraqi colleagues were also participating and sharing the danger and the difficult working conditions we and our families were living in Basrah, especially during busy periods at the front lines or the unpredictable shelling of the city, when large numbers of causalities were unpredictably admitted within hours.

CHAPTER 4

The Fear of the Iranians Occupying Our Hospital

Limitations & Challenges (Working Environment)

- Hospital staff & families risking their life
- Long Job Commitments
- Multiple injured patients & missed injuries
- Mass Casualties & Triage
- Other Medical & Surgical Emergencies.

WITH BASRAH BEING THE NEAREST and the largest border town to the Iranian border, it has always been at the risk of being taken over by the Iranian. Our teaching hospital was moved to another more peripheral hospital a few times during the war to be as far as possible from the range of the Iranian shelling.

There were times when we had nightmares about being taken as hostages by the Iranian because their forces kept advancing towards

Iraq after they regained the land they first lost to the Iraqi army at the beginning of the war. Our fears intensified every time we heard the shelling on the city and especially when our hospital itself was bombarded by the Iranian; a few patients in the intensive care unit were injured.

I and my colleagues discussed many times how to fled from the Iranians rather than be taken as hostages, when they were advancing towards the city of Basrah. We even discussed the option of getting down to the ground from the hospital's eight floors (neurosurgical unit was at the sixth floor), climbing down on multiple bed sheets tied to each other. One of my surgical colleagues remembered me reminding everyone to drive home in convoys of three or four cars at the end of our work shift in case one of us was injured from the unpredictable shelling.

NATIONAL DUTY, BUT HELPLESS AND RESENTFUL, WITH ACCEPTANCE OF GOD'S DECISION

Consultants, colleagues, nursing staff, and everyone looking after the wounded victims from what became a very long war had mixed feeling. I remained the only Iraqi neurosurgery consultant in Basrah until the end of the war.

A major general in the Iraqi army whom I met during war when he came to visit one of his injured officers at the hospital told me that the reason he escaped death countless times during active confrontation with the Iranian army was probably because "God has destined me to stay alive for a reason that I will never know". I, surgical colleagues, and all members of the medical staff probably had the same feeling while looking after the war-injured victims we saw every day for eight years, especially when some of our colleagues or members of their family were killed or injured from the Iranian shelling on the city, and each one of us wondered whether we were going to be next on the waiting list. We were helpless and resentful.

Like my colleagues and other surgeons in the hospital, it was always gratifying when we saved lives and the wounded recovered fully. Alas, as a neurosurgeon, sadly this was rarely the case with penetrating missile head or spinal injuries. Many of them died after surgery from the severity of their injuries, such as by sniper bullets at the front lines of the war, or they recovered with permanent disability. Missile or bullet injuries to the brain or the spine cause more devastating injuries and death than injuries to other parts of the body, as exemplified in the attached pie chart.

Even worse is my depression when they die before their turns come to be operated upon, due to the limited facilities in the hospital and lack of theatre space. when large numbers of wounded are admitted suddenly following a major battle at the front lines of the war zone or when the city is bombarded heavily by bombs falling on a school or a busy market.

Like all wars, I and my colleagues always felt that this tragic loss of lives and lifelong disabilities in young people would not have happened if it weren't for the irresponsible, stupid decisions by the rulers who could have avoided going to war, or at least stopped it early rather than insisting for it to continue for eight years with the wishful thinking that victory was imminent when they won one battle along the border and gained extra land from the other side, only to lose it again few months or weeks later. We were all paying the price for their decision.

NO PATIENTS' RELATIVES AND "NO CONSENT"

Because the injured soldiers come from different cities of Iraq and with no available contact details of their families most of the time, they were relocated quickly on the front lines of the war according to the needs of the battle. With the absence of mobile phones in those years, and especially with the quick turnover of the casualties we received and the large numbers admitted within a few hours, sometimes we simply had no time to get their families involved in the decision making about surgery. Victims simply had to trust their surgeons' decisions to operate or not and what operation they would perform. Many of my patients were unconscious from severe head injuries and could not give consent anyway.

THE RISK TO OUR LIVES AND THE GENERAL SURGEON KILLED IN THE HOSPITAL GROUNDS BY IRANIAN SHELLING

Civilians living in Basrah have always been at risk of being killed or injured by the unpredictable shelling. Mr Kais Abdulmajeed was a very unfortunate consultant general surgeon with the British fellowship who was posted from Baghdad to spend two weeks in Basrah as part of the contributions by other surgeons from all over Iraq. They were ordered by the ministry of health to share the suffering and the risk to the lives of those working in Basrah to raise their morale. He was instantly killed by shell fragments from an Iranian bomb which dropped in the hospital grounds as he was on his way to have supper in the dining room of the hospital staff.

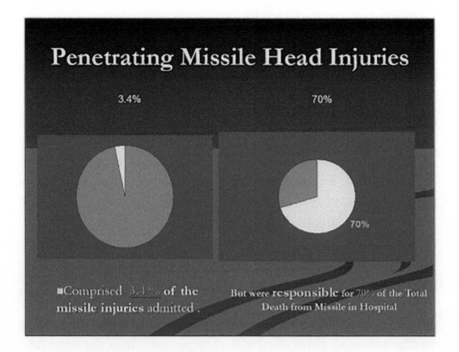

THE MOST DIFFICULT TIMES DURING THE WAR

The most challenging and difficult times during the war that I and all medical staff involved in the emergency treatment of the war victims (including my colleagues in other surgical specialities, the theatre nurses and assistants, and the anaesthetists), civilians from the shelling of the city, or army recruits from the war zone were being called to attend the hospital immediately because large numbers of casualties from the front lines had suddenly arrived through the hospital door. In the meantime, the city was being bombarded from the Iranian side, so we had to balance the two conflicting issues of reaching the hospital as soon as possible and risking our lives driving to the hospital when we could get killed or injured by the indiscriminate shelling of the city. I remember very well when a theatre assistant was killed by shell fragments in the hospital car park after he had just parked his car. Another one was killed as he drove his motorbike out of the hospital at the end of his shift.

Such a difficult and challenging situation occurred repeatedly during the eight years of the war, and we argued with whoever was the hospital director at the time about how to balance the two issues, but none of them had a clear answer. One hospital director called me out for being late in reaching the hospital while I was waiting for the shelling to quieten down before I drove. He senselessly argued that the chance of being killed or injured from the shelling on my way to the hospital was very minimal because it needed the coincidence of the shell falling exactly on me at the time I was driving!

My answer was that first of all, I could not risk the only life and the only body I had. Second, this coincidence of timing was what happened to all the victims I was going to treat, whether they were civilians or army recruits. Third, it was not easy to find a replacement neurosurgeon if I was injured or killed.

THE OPHTHALMOLOGIST WHO WENT TO PRISON

As a display to show that the regime was very serious and caring for the wounded, particularly the army recruits from the front line, surgeons could get punished if they ever neglected treating the wounded to the best of their abilities.

A wounded soldier was brought to the hospital with multiple fractures and scattered soft tissue injuries, including missile fragment injury to one of his eyes. To the bad luck of the ophthalmologist on call, he could not be contacted on time because he was in his private clinic. By the time he arrived at the hospital, the wounded patient had already been woken up from the anaesthetic and sent to the ward following treatment of his other multiple injuries. He was operated upon the next morning for his eye injury by the ophthalmologist, who was later sent to prison for a few months as a punishment for the late surgery.

MILITARY IMPLICATIONS OF THE WAR

The Iran–Iraq war was not only the longest war in the twentieth century. It was also the last conventional war in history. Most of the war routine was made of armoured and infantry battles, artillery and air strikes.

However, in two aspects, this war signalled a new era. Iraq first used its home-produced chemical weapons against the Iranian army with very limited impact. In March 1988, the Iraqi air force bombarded the Kurdish town of Halabja, killing three to five thousand people, which is the biggest chemical attack on civilian target in Middle Eastern history so far. With world inactivity, it gave the Iraqi regime a strategic advantage over the Kurds and encouraged the development of more unconventional capabilities.

In late 1987, Iraq modified the Soviet Scud B missile to extend its range. The two countries made use of long-range aircraft and ballistic attacks on cities and economic infrastructure throughout the war.

However, the active use of long-range missiles by Iraq in February 1988 contributed significantly to the Iranian surrender and ushered the Middle East into a ballistic era, affecting not only the Gulf but also the Arab-Israeli conflict.

ECONOMIC IMPLICATIONS OF THE WAR

Economically, the rising Iraqi economy of the 1970s, benefitting from the nationalisation of oil in 1972 and reaching a record oil production of 3.3 million barrels per day (BPD) by early 1980, plummeted within a year to 0.8 million BPD as a direct result of the war. Only in 2012 did Iraq reach its pre-war production levels. War costs weighed heavily on the Iraqi economy, which was now unable to pay for imports. At the end of the war, Iraq accumulated an external debt of over one hundred billion dollars. War strained Iraq's manpower: in addition to the estimated 180,000 casualties and 340,000 wounded, at the end of the war, the Iraqi army comprised of 1.2 million soldiers out of a population of 18 million.

The war dwindled the global and regional production of oil. Iran and Iraq, major producing countries and members of OPEC, were not able to reach pre-war production levels. Oil prices rose significantly. Though Saudi Arabia was the uncontested largest producer of oil, its oil industry, situated very close to the war front and export lines, was affected by the continuation of the war. In fact, the war affected the oil production all over the Gulf area. Since 1987, the "tanker war" expanded to include tankers exporting oil from other Gulf countries. This was an Iranian initiative intended to stop Gulf support to Iraq. Instead, it led to the first massive American military deployment in the area to protect Gulf tankers from Iranian attacks.

The Iran–Iraq war was the first major regional conflict in the Gulf that turned into a real war. It showed how sensitive and vulnerable Gulf oil was and how dangerous overreliance on it could be. In this sense, the war contributed to efforts to diversify sources of oil production worldwide

War profits, especially by arms suppliers to the two belligerents, were not much of a benefit. Iran and Iraq accumulated foreign debts, which they were unable to pay once the war ended. This had a devastating influence on major suppliers such as the USSR and its proxies. This may partially account for these countries' post-war economic and political collapse. Other countries providing economic and financial support, primarily Saudi Arabia and Kuwait, lost billions of dollars on loans to Iraq which have never been reimbursed.

REGIONAL IMPLICATIONS OF THE WAR

The war (Wikipedia) shifted the world's attention in the Middle East from the Arab-Israeli conflict to the Gulf region. It took Iraq out of any possible organisation of an "Eastern Front" in a war against Israel. In fact, with the signing of peace between Egypt and Israel, the planning of an "Eastern Front" against Israel became practically impossible. Thus, the Iran–Iraq war contributed indirectly to Israel's security. The war dismantled the axis of radical Arab countries that included Iraq, Libya, Syria and south Yemen. During the war Iraq shifted out of the radical camp to align with Egypt, Jordan, and the Gulf countries, while Syria remained Iran's sole Arab ally.

In the Gulf region, war reiterated the extreme vulnerability of all the Arab Gulf countries. Therefore, the war hastened a process of increasing interstate cooperation, mostly within the Gulf Cooperation Council. Under the direct threat from Iran and the potential future threat from Saddam's Iraq, the Gulf countries relied more heavily on

American military might, which consequently increased dramatically toward the war's end.

Farther north, the war helped Turkey attain regional supremacy. Stable after years of domestic strife and economically prosperous, Turkey made use of its geopolitical location during the war. By allowing Iraq to lay a major pipeline on its territory, Turkey provided an alternative to the Gulf route and became Iraq's main economic gateway. Turkey showed that oil and gas could be exported from the Gulf through its territory without using tankers.

The conflict has been compared to World War I in terms of the tactics used, including large-scale trench warfare with barbed wire stretched across fortified defensive lines, manned machine gun posts, bayonet charges, Iranian human wave attacks, extensive use of chemical weapons by Iraq, and, later, deliberate attacks on civilian targets. A special feature of the war can be seen in the Iranian cult of the martyr which had been developed in the years before the revolution. The discourses on martyrdom formulated in the Iranian Shi'a context led to the tactics of "human wave attacks" and thus had a lasting impact on the dynamics of the war.

An estimated 500,000 Iraqi and Iranian soldiers died, in addition to a smaller number of civilians. The end of the war resulted in neither reparations nor border changes.

CHAPTER 5

Was the Iraq Iran War Different from Other Long Wars?

EACH WAR IN THE WORLD has its own surgical problems; the principles of management of war wounds and war surgery have been described in most neurosurgery textbooks and military medical journals. The experience of World War II is considered the main source of knowledge about missile wounds in the time of war. The principles of management are based upon the experience of thousands of surgeons on millions of patients, and these surgical principles have successfully stood the test of time.

The Iran–Iraq war was characterised by quiescent periods most of the time, interwoven with periods of heavy fighting every now and then at the front lines or the indiscriminate shelling of Basrah City, which brought with them large numbers of causalities to our teaching hospital. Quite often the number of the injured casualties went far beyond the capacity of the operating theatres, available beds, medical and paramedical personnel, and hospital equipment.

The effect of artillery and rockets was responsible for the majority of injuries during combat or otherwise. The effect of air forces was limited on the Iraqi side because the Iranian air force was weaker and not efficient enough after the fall of the shah's regime. Bullet injuries during combat, commonly from snipers, were much less common and usually fatal when affecting the head.

The long, tortuous, uneven roads to Basrah city from the front line of the war at the Iraqi–Iranian border some twenty miles from the teaching hospital were responsible for much of the motor vehicle accidents we also received. These took place particularly at night because the roads were uneven, and often the mixture of plane and steep areas, coupled with the movement often being in complete darkness with vehicle lights turned off to avoid detection by the enemy (whether during action or otherwise), substantially increased the number of motor vehicle accidents. On the other hand, movement during the day made the troops more exposed to the artillery of the enemy.

During the war, many artillery shells from Iran fell on our teaching hospital itself and injured many inpatients in the intensive care unit. Hence, the neurosurgical unit was relocated twice to another peripheral hospital just outside the city centre to avoid the indiscriminate shelling. This happened apparently because the Iranians upgraded the range of their rockets, and it started reaching far areas away from the centre of Basrah.

Helmets were used only during the first few weeks of the war despite our continued instructions to keep using them. Their limited use was mainly due to the fact that the war continued for an unexpectedly long time, and partly to the very hot weather most of the year in southern Iraq and Basrah in particular, which made wearing them very uncomfortable.

PRINCIPLES OF TREATMENT OF PENETRATING MISSILE HEAD INJURIES

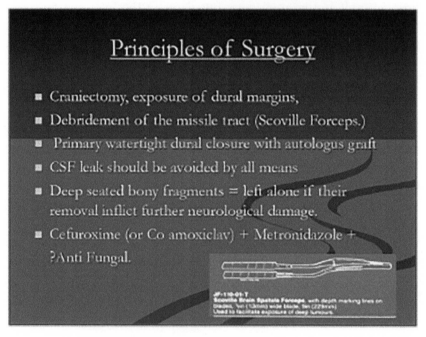

Missile head injuries, in contrast to missile injuries to other body parts, are rarely associated with significant blood loss unless they are associated with injuries to other body parts or a large scalp wound. The reason is the small size of the head compared to other body parts and the mechanism of clinical deterioration is quite different; the injured victim could die from the mass effect of an intracranial haematoma before any changes in blood pressure or pulse rate.

Harvey Cushing was the first to advocate early and definitive debridement of necrotic tissue, removal of all in-driven debris, and meticulous dural and scalp closure. He could reduce the operative mortality from 54 per cent to 28 per cent. During the early part of World War II and the Korean War, brain abscesses were routinely found in association with retained bone fragments. Because of this experience, aggressive initial debridement of the missile tract was adopted during the Vietnam War, and as a result the infection rate declined from 53 per cent to 15 per cent, and surgical mortality was also markedly reduced. Despite these results, the issue of the causal relation of retained bone fragments with the development of brain abscess remained speculative because there was evidence to the contrary.

With the availability of CT scans, rapid evacuation of casualties, and better follow-up neurosurgical care, a less aggressive intracranial debridement with emphasis to preserve the brain tissue was adopted during the Israeli, Lebanese, and Croatian conflicts, and the outcome was claimed to be better. Though great attention has been paid to brain injury, dural repair, and scalp closure, the treatment of fractured bone has been neglected.

THE DIFFERENCE IN THE MECHANISM OF BLUNT HEAD INJURIES AND PENETRATING MISSILE HEAD INJURIES

In the case of blunt head trauma, primary brain damage occurs at the moment of injury and consists mainly of contusions and diffuse axonal injury. In cases of severe head injury, it is followed by what is known as secondary damage, which can be considered as a complication of the original injury and includes intracranial haematoma, brain damage secondary to raised intracranial pressure, shift and herniation of the brain, brain swelling, and hypoxic brain damage

In the case of penetrating missile head injuries, the extent of the damage to the brain is proportional to the energy released by the penetrating bullet or missile fragment when it enters the brain. This energy is equal to half of the mass multiplied by the square of the velocity of the penetrating object (i.e., the energy will be quadrupled when the velocity has doubled).

$$E = 1/2 \text{ Mass} \times \text{velocity}^2$$

Another main difference between the two kinds of injuries is that penetrating missiles cause cavitation and shock waves, resulting in distant damages in the brain far away from the tract of the missile fragment or the bullet. This is unlike the cases of blunt trauma, where the extent of the damage will be limited to the site of impact or sometimes on the contralateral side, by what is known as contrecoup injury.

WHAT IS THE SHRAPNEL INJURY?

It is interesting to know that when I lectured about my experience in treating war injuries in many countries, I found very few people, or none, in the audience who know where the word *shrapnel* comes from.

Henry Shrapnel (1761–1842) (Wikipedia) is the British Army officer who invented an anti-personnel shell that transported a large number of bullets to the target before releasing them, at a far greater distance than rifles could fire the bullets individually.

INITIAL TREATMENT

Nearly all patients were brought to the hospital by ambulance, and most reached the unit within four hours of injury. The delay in evacuation of the wounded was due partly to the battle conditions and partly to the long distance from the frontline, sometimes over unpaved road. Only a few of the patients (the high-ranking military officers) were evacuated by helicopter. The number of patients received daily was unpredictable, and although there were many incidences of more than ten patients arriving within a few minutes, nearly all patients who required neurosurgical intervention were operated upon within twenty minutes of arrival at the hospital except when all theatres were occupied.

The lack of CT scans and angiography partly contributed to the speed of the surgery. Most of the casualties received little initial treatment apart from wound dressing, and care was often needed for concomitant injuries, the establishment and maintenance of an adequate airway, and the administration of intravenous infusions.

The patients were brought immediately to the emergency room at the ground floor, where their condition was evaluated, further resuscitation was performed, and surgical priorities for the injured organs were decided. Laparotomy was often performed before treatment of the head wounds in conscious patients with evidence of internal haemorrhage. Whilst still on the stretcher, X-ray films of the skull and other regions were taken as indicated. On most occasions, more than one doctor was available in the casualty department: one doctor would examine, record, and determine the priorities for management, and another would set up an intravenous infusion. Often an anaesthetist was called in to cope with the airway, which in some cases was the most important part of the initial management. In severely injured patients, placing the patients in a semi-prone position and inserting an airway often proved inadequate, and immediate tracheal intubation was often the only means of clearing the upper airway passage. Urinary catheters and nasogastric tubes were inserted at the same time in many cases.

In busy periods, selection of cases for operation was of the utmost importance (hence the preliminary examination being brief). This was at the expense of missing many injuries because the assessment had to be quick. The level of consciousness, state of pupils, movements of the limbs, and blood pressure were recorded, as well as rapid examination of the head wound and other injuries. In the shocked unconscious patients, immediate transfusion or restoration of adequate pulmonary ventilation took precedence over other treatment or investigation. Simple head dressings usually controlled the bleeding from scalp wounds, however this bleeding often starts again when the dressing was removed to inspect the wound in the casualty department.

Following resuscitation, stabilisation, and more immediate life-saving measures (operations for thoracic and vascular wounds, etc.), neurosurgical wound toilet and repair was performed. Often this was done concomitantly with other procedures or immediately following the other operation, while the patient was still under anaesthetic.

THE OPERATIVE TECHNIQUE

All cases with radiological evidence of penetrating missile injury (apart from the moribund and those showing clear signs of brain death) had operations. The scalp was widely shaved when the patient was anaesthetised to allow for any necessary extension of the entrance wound, especially if a rotation flap was thought to be necessary.

Retraction of the wound edges to expose the fracture site was helpful in deciding the direction in which to extend the wound, which was usually irregular. In tangential injuries, the bony defect often lies beneath an intact scalp farther away from the scalp wound, so it helps to palpate the wound first with a sterile glove to decide which direction to extend the incision.

The margins of the bony defect were then defined, and circumferential craniectomy was performed to remove the contaminated bone surrounding the site of the injury as well as to expose the dura. The dural opening nearly always needs to be enlarged to provide a better view of the underlying brain.

An intact pulsating dura mater need not be opened; if the dura was torn, quite often the edges had retracted, and the free graft was nearly always needed to achieve a satisfactory closure. On the whole, I found it essential to use a dural graft from the nearby pericranium or temporalis fascia without which watertight dural closure cannot be achieved because the dura retracts following the injury. Pulped brain, haematoma, and indriven bone fragments were removed by gentle suction and fine forceps. The preoperative X-ray films were frequently consulted to determine the depth of the indriven bone fragments. An image intensifier and Roper-Hall metal foreign body locator were often used to localise the metallic fragments if they seemed accessible and in the same hemisphere, and if their removal would not inflict further functional damage.

THE TECHNIQUE DESCRIBED BY ALAN CROCKARD IN *OPERATIVE NEUROSURGERY*

Alan Crockard recommended making a bur hole first to elevate the depressed bone fragments as in cases of depressed skull fracture caused by blunt trauma, which I found unnecessary and unacceptable, especially given that the mechanism of injury is quite different in the two types of head injuries, as one can tell from their names. One is simply "depressed skull fracture" and with intact dura in the majority of cases, whereas missile injuries are mostly "penetrating" and cause dural defect, which very often needs to be enlarged to remove the indriven bone fragments. Turning a rotation flap and performing a nearby burr hole was needless and impractical, particularly during busy periods when large numbers of casualties were admitted within a short time.

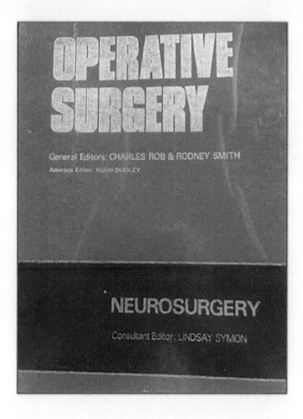

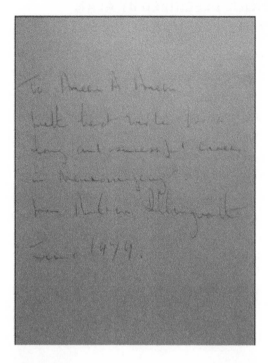

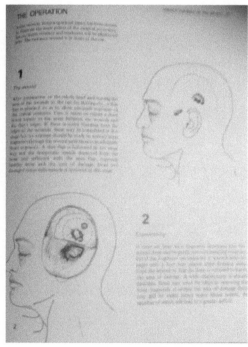

MY SURGICAL INPUT IN TREATING MISSILE HEAD INJURIES

Before I left my registrar job at the Central Middlesex Hospital, Robin kindly gave me an operative surgery book edited by Charles Rob and Rodney Smith. The neurosurgery section was written by Alan Crockard from his experience in Belfast, describing the operative procedure of treating missile head injuries. Mr Crockard recommended performing a burr hole opening away from the entrance of the missile, to be used for elevating the large, depressed bone piece at the entrance wound of the missile (as in the case of non-missile depressed skull fracture). I found this unnecessary and impractical, especially during busy periods, because it prolonged the operation time, increased the risk of infection by enlarging the craniectomy surgical wound, and created another bony defect with additional cosmetic difficulty. A depressed bone fragment can be elevated by minimal nibbling of the bony margins of the cranial defect made by the missile or by the blunt trauma to create a space for the insertion of the Adson's bone elevator to lift the depressed bone fragments. This procedure is not technically difficult and certainly avoids the need to make the additional burr hole as described by Mr Crockard.

In fact, in the majority of cases with penetrating missile head injuries, the bone fragments get indriven deep into the brain tissue and do not require an additional burr hole to extract them because they have to be looked for within the damaged and quite often necrotic brain tissue.

The bony defect made by the missile is usually large enough to insert the right sized bone nibbler and start the circumferential craniectomy. This method leaves the patient with one bony defect rather than the two recommended by Alan Crockard.

The hole made in the dura by the missile is rarely sufficient to allow full exploration of the underlying tract and thorough surgical debridement. Full inspection of the underlying damaged brain can be improved by retracting the brain surface from the torn dura with simple retraction of the dural edges away from the brain surface, with stay sutures attached to the pericranium.

In the majority of cases I treated, it was necessary to open the dura more along its torn edges. Retracting the dura with stay sutures up to the pericranium was often needed to improve visibility and access to the underlying damaged brain. The edges of the dural opening usually retract after a missile head injury, possibly by the heat liberated by the missile fragment, making it larger than those resulting from non-missile head injury.

Introducing the Scoville double blade brain retractor is very helpful to explore the missile tract and extract any debris, necrotic brain, and indriven bone fragments—and often the missile fragment(s) itself when accessible—especially when the surgeon works single-handedly.

Extending the dural opening would increase the difficulty of the recommended watertight dural suturing, which in my experience usually cannot be performed without a patch. I have used pericranium, temporalis fascia, galea, and rarely fascia lata from the thigh (for large defect), and I found them all to be very satisfactory in achieving the watertight closure to prevent CSF leakage and meningitis. I haven't used artificial dura because I think it is unnatural, could create a foreign body reaction, and more susceptibility to infection, in addition to the fact that it is expensive.

WIDE SKULL BASE FRACTURE AND DEEP MISSILE FRAGMENTS

I treated many cases with badly comminuted fracture of the floor of the anterior cranial fossa and open frontal sinus primarily with a dural graft rather than waiting for CSF rhinorrhoea to develop. The extensive defect (often bilateral) usually needs a large piece of fascia lata taken from the thigh. This would avoid the patient having a second operation to repair the dural defect. This contradicts the description in Hammon's report where he states, "At no time was it necessary to seek a dural graft elsewhere than from the cranial area."

The application of Roper-Hall metal foreign locator in conjunction with the image intensifier is often more helpful than using either one alone. Its role in this field has not been described before.

Extensive searching for removal of indriven bone and metallic fragments is not only unnecessary but may cause further damage.

The metallic fragments usually pass deeper than infected debris and bone fragments, and they do not necessarily follow the same track.

They are usually considered inaccessible if their removal would inflict further functional neurological damage.

Bullets and other large metallic fragments tend to wander within the brain because of their weight and remain a potential source of infection or further damage for years.

Brain abscesses are less likely to form around metallic than bone fragments. They usually occur within three to five weeks with reported incidents of 13–16 per cent, and they have been reported to occur up to thirty-eight years later.

In layman's terms, the retained missile fragments in an individual's brain cause apprehension, and it was difficult to reassure such individuals that attempting their removal could inflict further functional damage, especially when they are inaccessible; hence, I would perform repeat check-up X-rays to exclude migration. The situation is different with the few cases of retained bullets in the brain because they are much heavier than the common small metallic fragments, and they are known to migrate, even down through the foramen magnum to get lodged in the spine.

NEW CONCEPT IN THE REPAIR OF THE CRANIAL DEFECT

The principles of bone grafting were known to John Hunter more than two hundred years ago. Hunter determined that in the healing of fractures, bone was formed by the growth of vascular cellular tissue from surrounding muscles and periosteum and from bone ends themselves. He knew that in this process of repair, it was possible for bone fragments (completely stripped of all soft tissue attachments) to be incorporated in the mass of newly formed bone and even contribute towards union by bridging the fracture. But Hunter did not establish bone grafting as part of a surgical technique; he was defeated by sepsis.

During the eight years of the Iran–Iraq War, there were increased numbers of cranial defects resulting from war injuries. This invariably brought recurrent interest in this intriguing subject which at other times has been neglected. Past reports reveal surprising success with variable materials and methods generally whenever possible autogenous bone grafting was the procedure of choice. Of these, outer cranial table and ribs were referred to be used, but not primarily as in missile head injuries. Experience with this method reported here has not been reported with missile injuries before.

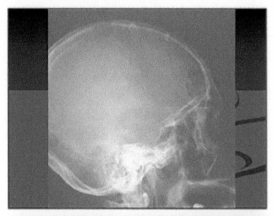

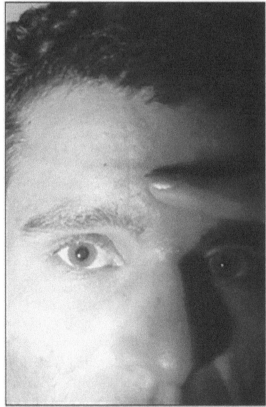

The healed frontal wound from the case above.

The common surgical practice in missile wounds is to discard all bone fragments from the craniectomy of the entrance wound because of their potential risk of infection. This very often results in an area of depression in the skull that is quite often ugly when at the frontal or temporal region, even with a hairy scalp. To avoid such an unsightly defect and the need for future cranioplasty, I reported my experience in 1986 of replacing the fractured bone pieces in a mosaic pattern as free bone grafts over the watertight closed dura (using pericranium, temporalis fascia, or fascia lata graft). In fifty-three selected cases of craniectomy for penetrating missile head injuries treated with debridement of missile tract followed by this procedure, only two cases developed signs of local wound infection, which was treated successfully with IV antibiotics. I applied this procedure only on selected patients who fulfilled the following criteria:

1. Must have been admitted within less than four hours from being wounded,
2. Had no obvious contamination of their wounds with dirt.
3. For the purpose of follow-up, only those living in Basrah and surrounding areas were chosen.

The procedure involves discarding the grossly contaminated bone pieces obtained from nibbling the immediate margins of the bony defect.

Unfortunately, long-term follow-up of the injured causalities could not be achieved because the military recruits were continuously relocated to other parts of the country.

Cases selected include those with bony defects which were too small to be considered for a full cranioplasty operation but too large to be ignored, and those in the cosmetically visible frontal region.

Although there have been many reports on the successful use of replacing the bony defect with depressed skull fracture due to non-missile injuries with fractured bone pieces, this method has not been reported before with penetrating craniocerebral injuries caused by missiles. In fact, the views expressed in previous reports on the subject were that replacement of bony fragments was never justified. Jeanett and Miller reported that missile head injuries "cause a degree of fragmentation and contamination that might make bone replacements impractical". The method I applied essentially involves the application of the fractured bone pieces resulting from the injury and the subsequent craniectomy in a mosaic pattern on the watertight closed dura, usually with the help of a pericranial patch after washing them with normal saline and discarding the grossly contaminated bone pieces. This is done as a primary procedure immediately after the debridement and dural suturing, and it has only been used in cases that arrive to the unit within four hours from wounding. I used this method in fifty-three patients, and only two developed early wound infection; they were treated by vigorous IV antibiotics for two weeks and eventually discharged. The remaining fifty-one patients achieved sound wound healing. The relatively long-term results of the thirty-seven patients who presented themselves for follow-up twelve to sixteen months post-operatively revealed good incorporation of the bone fragments with the solid skull and no signs of infection. Hence, the need for a second operation of cranioplasty with its attending risks was avoided. The patients chosen were those living locally in Basrah or its periphery because we were unable to follow those who were from outside Basrah. I published my results and technique in the *American Journal of Neurological and Orthopaedic Medicine and Surgery* in 1986 after presenting it at the Ninth Annual Meeting of the American Academy of Neurological and Orthopaedic Surgeons in 1985.

PENETRATING INJURIES INVOLVING BOTH CEREBRAL HEMISPHERES

These injuries are known to be associated with high mortality, and the actual extent of surgery bears little effect on the very poor prognosis. I came across six cases of bullet injuries involving both cerebral hemispheres (frontal or temporal lobes) who survived with minor or no obvious neurological deficits. In all cases, the bullet was removed from the other side via a second craniotomy, after the initial debridement of the entrance wound.

Bullets because of their heavy weight very often change their position within the soft brain, causing more damage, a fresh x-ray is needed in the theatre after positioning the patient, who is often prone. The bone flap is usually centred over the expected site of the bullet site, and adhesions between dura and the brain or evidence of fresh reactionary changes of the brain surface are guides for the site of the bullet.

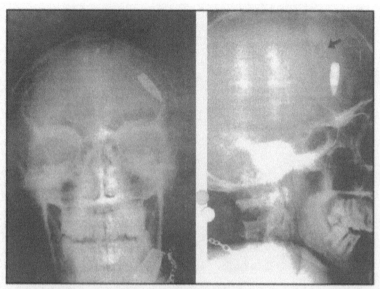

Bifrontal bullet injury. The arrow points to the skull entrance on the contralateral side.

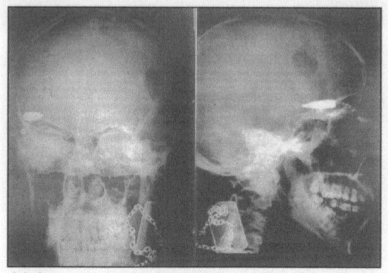

Debridement craniectomy performed on the entrance wound. Then the bullet was extracted from the opposite side. Note change of position of the bullet within few days.

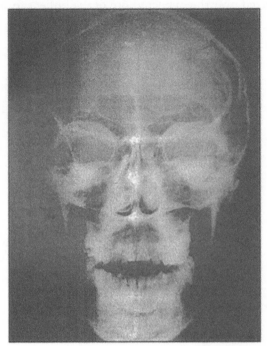

Skull x-ray after the bullet extraction.

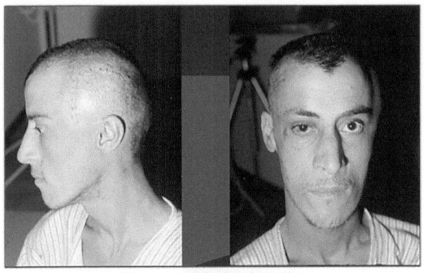

The patient recovered with no obvious deficit.

The first paper I published from my work in Basrah was in the *British Journal of Trauma Injury* in 1984 (16: 88–90), entitled "The Management of Acute Craniocerebral Injuries Caused by Missiles— Analysis of 110 Consecutive Penetrating Wounds from Basrah".

The series of 110 consecutive patients I treated represented my work over a six-month period. I reported that although penetrating missile head injuries comprised 3.4 per cent of the missile injuries admitted to our teaching hospital, either directly or transferred from nearby hospitals, those who died accounted for approximately 70 per cent of the total deaths in hospital from missiles. This clearly emphasised the seriousness of head injuries when compared to injuries to other body parts. I tried many times to bring this figure to the attention of the Ministry of Health and the Ministry of Higher Education to stress the importance of installing the CT scan, but this fell on deaf ears, and the unit remained without a working CT scan until I left Basrah in 1992.

The three points I emphasised in that paper are as follows. First, less-than-rapid evacuation determines those patients who are probably going to survive anyway. Second, bullet wounds of the head are nearly always fatal, especially if inflicted by high-velocity weapons. Third, the operation should include wide exposure of the injured site, thorough excision of the wound track, and watertight closure of the dura.

Out of the 110 consecutive patients admitted to Basra Teaching Hospital within six months, ninety- nine of them were caused by fragments of shells and eleven were by bullets. Of the ninety-nine patients admitted, eighty-nine underwent neurosurgical debridement procedures, and ten did not because they were moribund on admission due to the severity of their brain injury, and they died within a few minutes to a few hours after admission. They showed very slight or no response to pain, and they had fixed pupils. Seven had missile tracks crossing to the other hemisphere.

Because we were not allowed to disclose the number of the war-injured casualties we treated for security reasons, taking the example of 110 injured victims admitted under my care within six months as a guiding sample, I would roughly estimate that I must have looked after nearly 1,760 casualties during the eight years of the Iran–Iraq war, out of whom I must have operated on approximately 1,424 of them. Of all the patients admitted over this period, the mortality rate was 11 per cent.

The sites of the cranial penetration, the complications I had, and the number of associated injuries, together with the disabilities in the survivors, were published in my article in *Injury* in 1984.

The other points I emphasised in the management of penetrating cranial injuries are thorough debridement and removal of all indriven bone fragments, debris, and accessible metallic fragments, followed by watertight dural closure. These essential steps were followed in all penetrating missile head injuries I treated during the war. The intact dura not only is a strong barrier for infection but also reduces the risk of CSF fistula and prevents further necrosis of the brain from herniation through the defect. Reflection of the scalp for later cranioplasty would be much easier if the torn dura has been repaired because of the restoration of the normal anatomical dural covering that would prevent the adhesion between the brain and the scalp. In almost all cases I operated upon, the dural defect needed graft to achieve watertight dural closure, usually taken from the pericranium, temporalis fascia, and fascia lata. I did not use any artificial dura, which became available in our hospital a few years later.

CHAPTER 6

Complications of
My Operations

FOLLOWING THE SURGICAL DEBRIDEMENT OF the penetrating missile injured victims, we could care for them for only a short time, except for the civilians who lived in Basrah, because of the limited number of beds in our hospital and the need to keep empty as many as we could in anticipation of receiving large numbers of casualties from the front line of the war. The full ward, dedicated to the neurosurgical cases, could accommodate near fifty beds at one time, and those operated upon needed to be evacuated as soon as possible to Baghdad (the nearest available neurosurgical centre in the country) as early as possible, even if the ward was not in anticipation of any unexpected influx of causalities from the war zone or from Iranian shelling. This has clearly limited my follow-up to the wounded I operated upon, although I saw the majority during the next morning's ward round prior to their departure by train to Baghdad.

During the war, Iraqi surgeons from all specialties used to meet about once yearly in Baghdad to discuss their experience in the management of the war-injured victims, in particular the rehabilitation treatment offered to those with major disabilities (e.g., those with amputated limbs, or the paraplegics from spinal injuries). We all felt very shameful to see young army recruits with lifelong disabilities for which we as surgeons can do nothing to help them.

When I met many of my neurosurgical colleagues in Baghdad in those meetings, I often teased them. They would see my complications from Basrah because we had to transfer them as soon as possible after surgery. I jokingly asked who would see their complications. That said, I knew that they sent many of their cases outside Iraq, particularly the high-ranking officers in the army or the very complex cases.

88   Injury (1984) 16, 88-90   *Printed in Great Britain*

The management of acute craniocerebral injuries caused by missiles: analysis of 110 consecutive penetrating wounds of the brain from Basrah

A. A. Ameen
Neurosurgical Unit, Basrah University, Iraq

COMPARISON OF MY SERIES WITH OTHER STUDIES

Most previous studies referred to the era before computerised tomography, which is similar to the situation I had in Basrah. I doubt whether CT scans would have contributed much to the immediate treatment of cases with clear radiological and clinical evidence of penetrating brain injuries, though its value cannot be denied in detecting any associated intracerebral hematoma, especially those farther away from the missile tracts or in the diagnosis of postoperative haematoma, oedema, and abscesses.

The 10 per cent of patients with missile head injuries treated without operation is lower in my series than the 16 per cent reported by Hammon in 1971. This is most likely due to the swifter evacuation in the latter, where approximately 95 per cent of the patients were taken to hospital by helicopter, so many of them reached the hospital more quickly (within thirty or sixty minutes, compared to nearly four hours in my series). The same reason could explain the lower incidence of associated injuries in my series. The operative mortality for missile fragment cases was not significantly different across the two series (9.5 per cent in Hammon's series compared with 11 per cent in my series). The same surgical principals were applied in both. The sites of cranial penetration and the incidence of postoperative complication are also similar.

MISSED INJURIES DURING THE WAR

These commonly occur in the war-injured victims who presented with multiple injuries and unconsciousness. The majority were peripheral nerve injuries caused by missile fragments imbedded in the soft tissue which could easily be missed, especially if scattered all over the body. They are more easily missed in severe penetrating head injuries because attention is usually directed towards the management of the more serious, life-threatening injuries (particularly in the unconscious victims due to severe head injury or hypovolemic shock when proper, thorough neurological examination has not been achieved on admission). My contemporary colleague Professor Thamer Ahmed Hamdan (consultant orthopaedic surgeon) has written many articles on orthopaedic missile injuries, highlighting in particular the issue of missed injuries especially when their entrance cannot be seen or detected easily, such as in the axilla.

MISSILE SPINAL INJURIES

These were much less common than missile head injury cases. In general, they require neurosurgical intervention only if the missile fragment or bullet settles in the spinal canal, causing dural tear or neural compression.

The interesting, rarely known cases, which I wasn't aware of before the war, are the many cases of spinal cord injuries and paraplegia caused by shock waves when the bullets or missile fragments travel near the spinal canal without actually traversing it or even causing bony injury to the spinal column itself (including the laminae, spinous process, transverse process, or the vertebral body).

CONCUSSIVE SPINAL CORD INJURY
SECONDARY TO SHOCK WAVE

I have looked after such cases in Iraq where the bullet or the missile fragments cause damage to the spinal cord even without penetrating the spinal canal. Concussive effects, heat, fractures, or vascular injury may cause the neurological damage. Bullet or shrapnel removal and laminectomy do not change the prognosis.

I looked after one such patient from Afghanistan when I worked in Birmingham. He became paraplegic with complete loss of sensation below the mid thorax, and he had a linear fracture in the lamina of the D5 vertebra. His MRI scan showed cord oedema and contusion above and below the D5 level. I debated the indication for dorsal laminectomy with my consultant colleague on call, who most likely would not have accepted my judgement that this was not a case for laminectomy or any spinal surgical intervention, that it was the shockwaves that caused the cord damage (as supported by the MRI scan), from the traversing bullet which settled below the lower margin of the contralateral scapula.

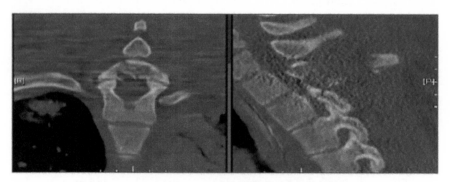

Laminar fracture only from traversing bullet injury,
causing paraplegia from the shock waves.

STRAY BULLET INJURIES

I treated many tragic cases of cranial bullet injuries caused by stray bullets falling down on the head during celebrations for various occasions or national festivals despite the strict government regulations and penalties imposed.

One unusual case was a bullet injury to the thoracic spine, causing paraplegia in an unfortunate young girl who was sleeping on the roof of their house at night, which was a known habit in many Middle East countries to escape the hot summer weather in their rooms, especially during the frequent power cuts.

CHAPTER 7

Difficult Times during the War

THE MOST CHALLENGING SITUATION WAS during busy periods when intense fighting at the front lines suddenly brought a large number of causalities requiring neurosurgical intervention. During the war's eight-year period, I experienced many such situations during my twelve-hour operating shifts when I quite often started with five patients waiting for surgery, and by the time I finish operating on one case, the waiting cases outside the theatre had increased to ten or more. I therefore had to continuously prioritise patients for surgery in the waiting area after each surgery.

Unfortunately, many patients died while waiting their turn to have surgical debridement procedures, mainly because of the limited facilities of two theatre rooms being available for head injury cases (and one of them was actually the anaesthetic room). Most of those who died while waiting for surgery were severely injured bullet injuries or fragment wounds who probably have been evacuated too swiftly.

HAPPY DAYS DURING THE WAR

During the eight-year period of the war, many clinical conferences and meetings were held in the Basrah Sheraton Hotel, mainly to assess the efficacy of the treatment we provided to the wounded victims. I took this opportunity to invite Robin Illingworth, Martin Rice Edwards, and Peter Stanworth from the UK for a short visit of a week or so to attend these meetings, participate in teaching activities to the undergraduate students, and examine some patients if and when they could.

THE SHOMAN AWARD FOR YOUNG ARAB SCIENTIST

The Abdul Hameed Shoman Foundation was established in 1978 by the Arab Bank, in what was then an innovative move by the private sector to contribute to the initiation of a beacon of knowledge and innovation in Jordan and the Arab world. Since its establishment, the foundation continues to play a positive role in enriching the Jordanian and Arab culture, as well as developing the scientific scene through knowledge, research, and dialogue.

The foundation's mission is to invest in cultural and social innovation to positively impact the communities it serves through thought leadership, arts and literature, and social innovation.

In recognition of my eight years' service in treating the wounded of the Iraq–Iran War, including the civilians injured from the shelling of the city; exposing myself to the risk of being killed or injured when moving between different hospitals sites; and the many articles I published about my experiences in the management of the war-injured casualties, I was granted this award in November 1988 in Amman, Jordan, which comprised a cheque of three thousand Jordanian dinar.

ROBIN ILLINGWORTH'S TWO VISITS TO IRAQ

Robin was the first one to accept the invitation from Basrah University, and he was delighted to see me waiting for him in Baghdad Airport. The bad news was when he was told that Iraqi Airways had left his luggage behind in Heathrow Airport, so he had to wait four days for the next flight to arrive from London. In some ways this was actually fortunate because I took him to do sightseeing in Baghdad and nearby areas, including Taq Kasra Ctesiphon (Persian for Iwan of Chosroes), which is the remains of a circa third- to sixth-century Sasanian-era Persian monument, sometimes called the Arch of Ctesiphon. It is located near the modern town of Salman Pak. He also visited the Islamic shrine in Khadimiah near Baghdad (the city where I was born) and enjoyed a quick lunch cooked by my late mother.

We visited Samarra, which is an archaeological city 124 kilometres north of Baghdad and the site of a powerful Islamic capital city. It is home to the famous spiral minaret as well as the golden shrines of two of the twelve Shi'a imams.

When Robin's baggage arrived on the next Iraqi Airways flight from London, we headed to Basrah in the car provided by Basrah University, and on our way we visited UR, which is known as an important Sumerian city-state in ancient Mesopotamia, with its famous Zakoora and other archaeological places. I kept telling Robin that we should thank Iraqi Airways for missing his luggage in London and giving us this opportunity of sightseeing for a few days.

In Robin's second visit to Basrah, the university also invited his anaesthetist colleague, the late Dr Maggie Hunt, and on the second day of their arrival to Basrah, we went with many members of the teaching staff in the Medical College for a boat trip to the Arab marshes. On our way to Basrah, we visited the archaeological site of UR. Robin's anaesthetist at the Central Middlesex Hospital, Maggie Hunt, said, "My life ambition has been fulfilled. I have seen the Zakkora."

PETER STANWORTH'S TWO VISITS TO BASRAH

Peter Stanworth is a consultant neurosurgeon in Coventry. As a lieutenant colonel, he joined the army in September 1959 and has served in the TA without a break since 1961 on operations and exercises across the world, including Gulf War One, Kosovo, Iraq, and Afghanistan. He was instrumental in introducing head injury workshops using pigs as models. He was the first neurosurgeon to be sent to Helmand Province in Afghanistan.

Peter's first visit to Basrah was to participate in our local educational conference sponsored by the university, in which I presented my experience in treating war-injured causalities. Peter participated in the teaching activities and also operated on many cases of missile head injuries during his two visits to Basrah.

It so happened that we received large numbers of causalities during the days of his visit, and I remember he was quite impressed by the operative capabilities of our surgical registrars, noting that they were probably quicker than him in performing the neurosurgical debridement procedures.

During his stay at Shat Al Arab Hotel, I was concerned about his safety, especially because the shelling on Basrah escalated for unknown reasons during his visit. Peter therefore moved to stay with us in my house for about a week.

I must say that I was surprised when he accepted our invitation for a second trip to Basrah, regardless of the risk of shelling on the city, which he had experienced during his first visit. This time he came with his wife, Janet.

The irony is that although Peter and I both worked on the same "surgical battlefield" in Basrah, treating Iraqi causalities from the Iraq–Iran War, a few years later in 1991, Peter was on the "other side" of the war when he came to Kuwait with the British army after Iraq invaded Kuwait!

PETER STANWORTH AND SIR VICTOR HORSLEY

During one of his two trips to Basrah, Peter and one of our junior doctors visited the cemetery of the British soldiers killed in Iraq during the wars in Amarah (ninety-five miles north of Basrah) and the memorial wall of Sir Victor Horsley (1857–1916), the pioneering British neurological surgeon who had passed away more than one hundred years ago. He died in his sixtieth year from the effects of heat stroke while serving as consulting military surgeon to the Mediterranean Expeditionary Force in Amarah city, south of Iraq, and was buried in the now largely abandoned Amara War Cemetery. By the time of his death in 1916, Victor Horsley had established himself as one of the most eminent innovators of modern neurological surgery.

Peter Stanworth with my three-year-old daughter at the entrance of Shatt Al Arab Hotel in Basrah (1986).

CHAPTER 8

Teaching Cases from the War Injuries

Any Advances ?

- Earlier + faster evacuation by air ambulance will detect more hematoma
- Understanding the pathology of head injury, refinements in operative technique + new monitoring equipments.
- aggressive antibiotic prophylaxis + avoidance of aggressive debridement has improved morbidity and mortality over the last 35 years.
- Early aggressive hemicraniectomy to accommodate brain swelling during the long overseas transport.

THE PATIENT WHO DIED ON THE TABLE

I CAN NEVER FORGET THIS case because it is the only patient in the whole of my neurosurgical career who died on the operating table while I was operating on him. This was a case of a large missile fragment which penetrated the lateral sinus (a sac of blood that runs laterally in a groove along the interior surface of the occipital bone) and settled with nearly half of it remaining outside the scalp. Taking the shell fragment out of the sinus was followed by torrential bleeding that was very difficult to stop and finally became fatal, despite preparing a pericranial patch beforehand to patch the defect in the sinus. Unfortunately, the large amount of blood transfusion given was not enough. Following this operation, I didn't stop thinking about the way I could have stopped this tragic death from happening. I felt that following the craniectomy, I should have started suturing the patch to the sinus wall just outside the dural defect, and I should have kept my finger on the patch to cover the sinus opening before extracting the missile fragment from the sinus because the pericranial patch kept being pushed by the large gush of bleeding from the sinus. Furthermore, in retrospect the anaesthetist also felt that the patient should have had many lines of blood transfusion at the same time.

HYSTERICAL BLINDNESS

This was an injured soldier admitted after being accused of faking his blindness to get away from military service, as many soldiers did when the war went on for many years with no apparent light at the end of the tunnel. The small entry wound of shell fragment in his occiput (the back of the head) was missed, concealed by his thick black hair. He was fully conscious but shouting that he couldn't see, to the disbelief of the medical staff around him. Shortly afterwards, simple skull x-rays solved the mystery by showing the small missile fragment of shell crossing from one occipital lobe of the brain (where the visual cortex is located) to the contralateral, clearly damaging both of his visual centres in the brain. The small, indriven bone fragments from the cranial entrance could hardly be seen.

BRAIN HYDATID CYST IN BASRAH

In the absence of CT scans in Basrah during the 1980s, I had little chance to operate on patients other than traumatic cases of head and spinal injuries. An eighteen year old patient was referred to me by the ophthalmologist who found bilateral papilledema causing his blurring of vision. I operated on him successfully when he returned from Baghdad with his CT brain scan showing the classical features of a hydatid cyst, which I hadn't seen in UK before I had left. The cyst was delivered intact into the kidney dish held below the head when his body was tilted downward and sideway to keep the cyst in the most dependent position, with gravity helping its intact delivery to avoid rupturing into the cranial cavity and regrowth of the hydatid; this was known as the Dowling technique, which I wasn't aware of before this case.

This case reminded me of the late David Utley, when I did a locum post at Atkinson Morley's Hospital in London. He used to say that he always thought of hydatid cyst with patients he saw from overseas, but he hadn't seen a single case yet!

Robin was interested in having copies of the operative photos I took for the case, which I later published in the British journal *Tropical Doctor* in 1986.

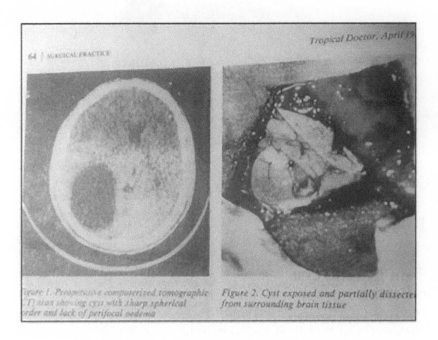

Figure 1. Preoperative computerized tomographic (CT) scan showing cyst with sharp spherical border and lack of perifocal oedema

Figure 2. Cyst exposed and partially dissected from surrounding brain tissue

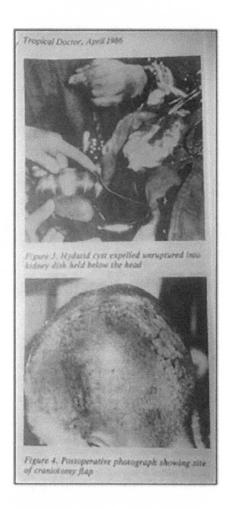

Figure 3. Hydatid cyst expelled unruptured into kidney dish held below the head

Figure 4. Postoperative photograph showing site of craniotomy flap

TEACHING ACTIVITIES

In recognition of the publication of many articles I published describing my years of experience on the neurosurgical management of missile head injuries in British and American journals, attending conferences abroad, and organising with my colleagues many local conferences in Basrah, as well as inviting three British neurosurgeons (including two visits by Robin, two by Peter Stanworth, and one by Martin Rice Edwards) and one general surgeon, I was promoted to assistant professor in Basra Medical College. I then became the head of the surgery department, with the extra duties of supervising teaching activities in the department. There were nearly thirty lecturers and consultants in different surgical specialties, including ophthalmology, ENT, orthopaedics, general surgery, cardiothoracic, and neurosurgery. I had the responsibility of overseeing written examination questions, correction of papers, and clinical exams. Such activities went hand in hand with my clinical commitments and the on-call duties for the war injured and other emergency neurosurgical admissions, as well as the elective neurological and neurosurgical cases admitted to our hospital.

STRESSFUL TIMES AND APPREHENSION

The most stressful time I experienced, like all civilians living in Basrah during the war's eight-year period, was the nervousness and fear with which we lived, panicking for our children's safety when they went to school during the indiscriminate and unpredictable bombardment on the city of Basrah. This bombardment targeted civilians anywhere and anytime, and it could occur unpredictably during the course of our ordinary daily lives. I had to move my children to Baghdad for many weeks to live with my sister, fearing for their safety during the periods of intense shelling.

CHAPTER 9

The Second Gulf War 1991: Operation Desert Storm (16 January 1991– 28 February 1991)

On August 2ND (Wikepedia) 1990, Iraqi forces invade Kuwait, Iraq's tiny, oil-rich neighbour. Kuwait's defence forces were rapidly overwhelmed, and those that were not destroyed retreated to Saudi Arabia. The emir of Kuwait, his family, and other government leaders fled to Saudi Arabia, and within hours Kuwait City had been captured and the Iraqis had established a provincial government. By annexing Kuwait, Iraq gained control of 20 percent of the world's oil reserves and, for the first time, a substantial coastline on the Persian Gulf. The same day, the United Nations Security Council unanimously denounced the invasion and demanded Iraq's immediate withdrawal from Kuwait. On August 6, the Security Council imposed a worldwide ban on trade with Iraq.

On January 16, 1991, Operation Desert Storm, the massive U.S.-led offensive against Iraq, began as the first fighter aircraft were launched from Saudi Arabia and off U.S. and British aircraft carriers in the Persian Gulf. All evening, aircraft from the U.S.-led military coalition pounded targets in and around Baghdad as the world watched the events transpire on television footage transmitted live via satellite from Iraq. Operation Desert Storm was conducted by an international coalition under the supreme command of U.S. General Norman Schwarzkopf and featured forces from 32 nations, including Britain, Egypt, France, Saudi Arabia, and Kuwait.

Early on the morning of 17, January, 1991, a massive U.S.-led air offensive hit Iraq's air defenses, moving swiftly on to its communications networks, weapons plants, oil refineries and much more. The coalition effort, known as Operation Desert Storm, benefited from the latest military technology, including stealth bombers, cruise missiles, so-called "Smart" bombs with laser-guidance systems and infrared night-bombing equipment. The Iraqi Air Force was either destroyed early on or opted out of combat under the relentless attack, the objective of which was to win the war in the air and minimise combat on the ground as much as possible.

WAR ON THE GROUND

By mid-February, the coalition forces had shifted the focus of their air attacks toward Iraqi ground forces in Kuwait and southern Iraq. A massive allied ground offensive, Operation Desert Sabre, was launched on February 24, with troops heading from northeastern Saudi Arabia into Kuwait and southern Iraq. Over the next four days, coalition forces encircled and defeated the Iraqis and liberated Kuwait. At the same time, U.S. forces stormed into Iraq some 120 miles west of Kuwait, attacking Iraq's armored reserves from the rear. The elite Iraqi Republican Guard mounted a defense south of Basrah in southeastern Iraq, but most were defeated by 27 February.

THE POST-WAR INDISCRIMINATE
KILLING BY SADDAM HUSSEIN

With Iraqi resistance nearing collapse, Bush declared a ceasefire on February 28, ending the Gulf War. According to the peace terms that Saddam Hussein subsequently accepted, Iraq would recognise Kuwait's sovereignty and get rid of all its weapons of mass destruction (including nuclear, biological and chemical weapons). In all, an estimated 8,000 to 10,000 Iraqi forces were killed, in comparison with only 300 coalition troops.

Though this war was recognised as a decisive victory for the coalition, Kuwait and Iraq suffered enormous damage, and Saddam Hussein was not forced from power.

Intended by coalition leaders to be a "limited" war fought at minimum cost, it would have lingering effects for years to come, both in the Persian Gulf region and around the world. In the immediate aftermath of the war, Hussein's forces brutally suppressed uprisings by Kurds in the north of Iraq and Shi'as in the south. The United States-led coalition failed to support the uprisings, afraid that the Iraqi state would be dissolved if they succeeded.

In the years that followed, U.S. and British aircrafts continued to patrol skies and mandate a no-fly zone over Iraq, while Iraqi authorities made every effort to frustrate the carrying out of the peace terms, especially United Nations weapons inspections. This resulted in a brief resumption of hostilities in 1998, after which Iraq steadfastly refused to admit weapons inspectors. In addition, Iraqi forces regularly exchanged fire with U.S. and British aircraft over the no-fly zone.

The initial conflict to expel Iraqi troops from Kuwait began with an aerial and naval bombardment on 17 January 1991, not only on Kuwait but also including Basrah and many other Iraqi cities. This bombardment continued for five weeks and was followed by a ground assault on 24 February. The coalition forces liberated Kuwait first and then advanced into Iraqi territory. The coalition ceased its advance and declared a ceasefire one hundred hours after the ground campaign started. In return, Iraq launched Scud missiles against coalition military targets in Saudi Arabia and in Israel.

Civilians in Basrah suffered the most from this war. An extraordinarily large number of causalities were admitted to Basrah's hospitals, mainly from the retreating Iraqi army withdrawing its forces from Kuwait. This was followed by many civilian casualties from the confrontation of Iraqi civilians with defeated army forces, in their attempt to topple the regime and Saddam Hussein after all the destruction he had caused. Life became very difficult because of the economic sanctions subsequently imposed on Iraq, which led to an extreme shortage of food and medicines.

With his well-known extreme brutality, Saddam Hussein did his best to crush the uprising of the Iraqi resistance movement and indiscriminately bombarded Basrah city. This caused extensive damage and destruction, capturing my family home at the time, which caught fire on its first floor while I was on duty at the hospital. My two young children miraculously escaped death; they had been in their room just a few minutes before the large shell went through it.

The management of the war's injured victims was not much different during this war than from those of the Iran–Iraq war. However, this time the treatment we provided was with much more experience, quicker, and more organised, with all parties involved having seen the worst not long ago.

Causalities from the Second Gulf War that we treated during these four days were minimal compared to those we received and treated during the eight years of the Iraq–Iran War.

CHAPTER 10

Post-withdrawal of the Iraqi Army from Kuwait

THE **HIGHWAY OF DEATH (WIKEPEDIA)** is a six-lane highway between Kuwait and Iraq, officially known as **Highway 80**. It runs from Kuwait City to the border town of Safwan in Iraq and then on to the Iraqi city of Basra. The road was used by Iraqi armored divisions for the 1990 Invasion of Kuwait.

American, Canadian, British and French aircraft and ground forces attacked retreating Iraqi military personnel attempting to leave Kuwait on the night of February 26–27, 1991, resulting in the destruction of hundreds of vehicles and the deaths of many of their occupants. Between 1,400 and 2,000 vehicles were hit or abandoned on the main Highway 80 north of Al Jahra.

The scenes of devastation on the road are some of the most recognizable images of the war, and it has been suggested that they were a factor in President George H. W. Bush's decision to declare a cessation of hostilities the next day. Many Iraqi forces successfully escaped across the hrates river, and the US Defence Intelligence Agency estimated that upwards of 70,000 to 80,000 troops from defeated divisions in Kuwait might have fled into Basra, evading capture.

The attacks became controversial, with some commentators arguing that they represented disproportionate use of force, saying that the Iraqi forces were retreating from Kuwait in compliance with the original UN Resolution 660 of August 2, 1990, and that the column included

Kuwaiti hostages and civilian refugees. The refugees were reported to have included women and children family members of pro-Iraqi, PLO-aligned Palestinian militants and Kuwaiti collaborators who had fled shortly before the returning Kuwaiti authorities pressured nearly 200,000 Palestinians to leave Kuwait. Activist and former United States Attorney General Ramsey Clark argued that these attacks violated the Third Geneva Convention, Common Article 3, which outlaws the killing of soldiers who "are out of combat. Clark included it in his 1991 report *WAR CRIMES: A Report on United States War Crimes Against Iraq to the Commission of Inquiry for the International War Crimes Tribunal.*

THE UNFORGETTABLE SHOOTING OF A JUNIOR DOCTOR IN THE HOSPITAL CAR PARK.

In Iraq, Saddam Hussein used war and emergency rules as a pretext to establish an unprecedented totalitarian dictatorship. He crushed and uprooted the organised Shiite opposition shortly before the war, thus denying the majority group in Iraq's population a tool for expressing their indignation. This allowed Saddam to rely on an army with a Shiite majority to fight Shiite Iran. Influenced by Stalin, Saddam presented the war as the Iraqi equivalent of the "Great Patriotic War" (World War II in Soviet parlance), producing some patriotic zeal even among Shiite warriors. The Iraqi Communist Party, previously a real challenge to the Baath, did not survive the purge in 1977 and ceased to be a real threat to the Saddam regime in the 1980s. For the Kurds, on the other hand, war was an opportunity to renew their rebellion. The Kurdish rebels established a new leadership and restarted the rebellion in the north.

In the middle of this totalitarian regime and dictatorship, we clinicians and treating surgeons operated on and looked after the causalities. We saw the horrific injuries especially affecting the young military recruits, and we can only praise their sacrifices and courage. On the other hand, we had to hide our feelings to remain safe, and we could never even whisper a word against the regime or the wrong decisions made by Saddam Hussein to take the whole country to a needless war when Iraq was unprovoked, costing so many lives and permanent disabilities on both sides—let alone the economic hardship and the consequences of halting the country's development and progress.

Criticising the regime in any negative way could risk our lives (and our families' lives) with Saddam's spies being everywhere. A secret detective could be any of our closest friends, or even a relative.

Dr Abdul Jabbar Al Bahadily was a junior resident who could not hide his hatred towards the regime and Saddam after the crushing defeat of the Iraqi army in Kuwait. He was brought up to Basrah Teaching Hospital's car park by the security officers a few days after they had crushed the anti-regime demonstration in Basrah. The doctor was shot in front of as many of the hospital staff as they could get at the time. He was left dead in the same spot for few more days as a reminder to everyone who dared to speak a word against the regime. I think this brutal attitude and ruthlessness was what kept Saddam Hussein in power for thirty-five years.

A similar scenario occurred at another main hospital in Basrah when two of the female hospital staff were shot in front of their colleagues in the hospital grounds because they smashed Saddam's portraits at the height of their anger after the Iraqi army's defeat in Kuwait.

MORE HORRIBLE ATROCITIES IN BASRAH

As if the shooting of hospital staff in front of their colleagues was not enough, many dead bodies of those who protested or demonstrated against the regime when the Iraqi army was defeated and withdrew from Kuwait were left exposed in the main roundabout of Basrah for many days, for everyone to see as a warning and a reminder to whoever dared to speak against the regime.

CHAPTER 11

Emigrating from Iraq in 1992

AFTER THE HORRORS OF THE Iran–Iraq War of the 1980s, the invasion of Kuwait, the Gulf War of 1990–1991, and the subsequent extensive UN sanctions imposed on Iraqi society during the 1990s, life became intolerable. Like many of my colleagues with British or American qualification and experience, emigration from Iraq was our best option, having served the country for more than a decade during the most difficult time and with no light at the end of the tunnel.

No one has a reasonable explanation as to why Iraq, with its eminent history and previously being the cradle of civilisation, descended to a very poor state in economy and education. There had been devastation from repeated wars and conflicts between stupid leaders fighting amongst themselves or against neighbouring countries (Iran and Kuwait) since 1958.

Despite being a wealthy country, Iraq's political instability since the 1958 revolution pushed many, including myself, to emigrate commonly to the UK or the United States after getting their university degrees, taking advantage of our undergraduate university study being in English language. I believe that those who remained in Iraq had strong family ties and perhaps wishful thinking that the country would be politically stable one day. Unfortunately, time has proven them wrong, as demonstrated by repeated upheavals and the frequent revolutions and coups.

Many Iraqis strongly believe that the country's instability, with repeated revolutions and coups, have been orchestrated by the British or the Americans, utilising the selfish feeling of many Iraqi politicians and army generals to become leader of the country. In the end, they believe that the aim was to keep Israel safe and stable.

Since my childhood, I recall two of my cousins who emigrated to the United States, one after qualifying from the secondary school and the second after getting his university degree. We sporadically get in touch with them every now and then.

The obligatory military service in Iraq at the age of eighteen or after completing university study also prompted many to emigrate as early as possible, especially because the service could extend for many years depending on the need of the army for more recruits, such as during the eight years of the Iraq–Iran War, during which three of my wife's relatives and two of her university colleagues were killed.

I and my wife were particularly worried about our only son, who was fourteen years old when I left Iraq. He was a few years away from being called to do the obligatory army service.

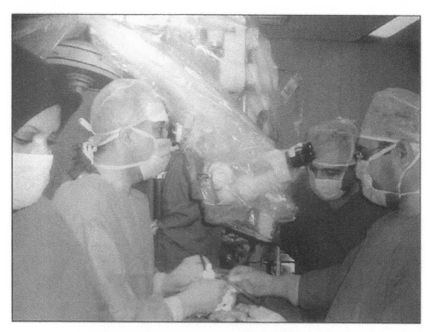

May 2006 in Basrah Teaching Hospital.

MOVING TO JORDAN FIRST, 1992

My family and I had miraculously survived the frequent clusters of shelling from the Iranian border, the horrific bombardment of Basrah city on 17 January 1991 after Iraq invaded Kuwait in August 1990, the indiscriminate shelling of the resistance movement when Iraqi forces withdrew from Kuwait, and the burning of our house. Life became intolerable to many who had the opportunity to emigrate—and staying became even more difficult with the hardship of the embargo imposed on Iraq after the invasion of Kuwait.

Like many of my consultant colleagues in the hospital or in the university, we felt that now we had good reasons to emigrate from Iraq, having fulfilled our national duties towards the wounded from the three wars in ten years. Now we had to face the crippling embargo and the economic hardship, especially with the severe depreciation of Iraqi currency: the average university professor started to receive a monthly salary of nearly ten dollars. We were looking for a better future for our children.

Family travelling outside Iraq was prohibited during the war because the government feared losing their expertise. Fortunately, I had the opportunity to move to a new role as a consultant neurosurgeon and associate professor at Jordan University Teaching Hospital in Amman for two years, with the advantage of being awarded in 1988 the Shuman Prize for Young Arab Scientists in clinical science for my clinical services during the war and the papers I published.

The facilities in Jordan University Hospital were more up-to-date than in Basrah, with the availability of CT and MRI scans and the opportunity to perform all the elective and emergency neurosurgical procedures that I could have performed if I would have stayed in the UK. Life and work were more fulfilling and enjoyable when compared to the twelve years I had spent in Basrah dealing mainly with war injuries, although I and my family missed the social life with our Iraqi families and friends in Basrah.

The medical staff at Jordan University Hospital were very kind and appreciative, especially my dear colleague, the clinical service lead, Professor Walid Maani, with whom I published two papers on head injuries during my two years of service.

In Amman, I and my family felt at home. Iraqis and Jordanians are very close socially to each other, partly from the nostalgia of their old kings being cousins: Hussein and Faisal the Second. The latter was killed in the coup of 1958.

In 1994, at the end of my two-year contract at Jordan University Hospital, I chose to re-emigrate back to the UK.

CHAPTER 12

Back to the UK Again in 1994

AFTER RETURNING TO THE UK in 1994, I moved between various neurosurgical posts, including Coventry (1995–1998) and Royal Free Hospital (1998–2006). My consultant colleagues Robert Bradford, Robert Maurice Williams, Colin Sheif, and Neil Dorward (who kindly introduced me first to the Royal Free Hospital) were very kind and supportive during those eight years I spent with them. I found all the nursing and clinical staff in both units to be very kind and supportive.

I then took my first early retirement at the age of fifty-eight with the kind support and help of Robert Bradford from the Royal Free Hospital.

After leaving my post at the Royal Free Hospital, I felt I could carry on working, utilising my twenty-one years' neurosurgical experience, so I accepted a three-year post as a senior consultant neurosurgeon in Hamad Medical Corporation, Doha, Qatar.

THREE-YEAR NEUROSURGERY POST IN QATAR, 2006–2009

In 2006, after having taken an early retirement from my eight-year post at the Royal Free Hospital in London, I accepted a senior consultant neurosurgeon role in Hamad General Hospital, Doha, Qatar, with three theatre sessions and two outpatient clinics a week. The unit is fully equipped with modern neurosurgical armamentarium (cusa, brain lab neuronavigation, vascular neurointervention, microscope, etc.).

All four Consultants in the unit and the juniors attend the daily handover morning meeting discussing the management of all admission and weekly neuroradiology and neuropathology meetings. The senior consultant neurosurgeon Ali Raza was very supportive, intelligent, and caring. The unit serves the whole

1.5 million population of Qatar, dealing with all acute and elective neurosurgical conditions, including pediatric neurosurgery.

The booming economy of the country with the build-up of huge towers brought with it large numbers of head and spinal injuries—thus the extra experience I gained in neurotrauma, including spinal fusion and severe blunt head injuries. The hospital had all the facilities of modern neurosurgical service (cranial and spinal).

Patients in the Middle East commonly have little faith in their national and private medical service, and the majority of people keep asking for another opinion, which could be three or four, until they are satisfied. On the whole, they are very appreciative of successful treatment and do their best to spread the good word, including the national newspapers, as in the two appreciation comments below from Jordan and Qatar:

Patients from Jordan and Qatar appreciating my service in the national newspapers.

ROBERT BRADFORD'S "ROYAL" CONSULTATION IN DOHA

A few weeks after starting my post in Qatar, a member of the royal family sustained a fractured lumbar spine for which I advised conservative treatment because he had no neurological deficit. A French surgeon came and advised spinal fusion, which I argued as being unnecessary and carrying known risks and complications. To support my view, they requested another UK surgeon whom I knew as a third opinion. Robert Bradford came to Doha and agreed with my view. When mobilised out of bed six weeks later and with the physiotherapy treatment he received, he became fully active and mobile. He went to Haj and did the seven rounds of running around Kaaba.

بسم الله الرحمن الرحيم

شكر وتقدير

بعد أن من الله تعالى على زوجتي (حليمة مصطفى البنا) بالشفاء اثر العملية الجراحية الكبرى التي اجرتها في مستشفى الجامعة الاردنية اتقدم بجزيل الشكر والعرفان الى الاطباء الافاضل الذين جعل الله تعالى على ايديهم الشفاء وهم:

الدكتور امين عباس (اخصائي جراحة الدماغ والاعصاب) والدكتور حميد المصري والدكتور هاني عبدالعزيز والدكتور عوني مشربش ودكتورة التخدير سحر حدادين ودكتور التخدير صبحي الغانم والى كافة الممرضين والممرضات في الطابق الثالث الذين قاموا بواجبهم على اكمل وجه. سلم الله هذه الايادي الذهبية وحفظ هذه العقول العلمية والله الموفق.

مصطفى البنا وعائلته

الشرق

شكر وتقدير

يتقدم الزميل محمد سقباني بجريدة الشرق الى الدكتور امين عباس امين كبير استشاريي الأعصاب بمستشفى حمد بالشكر الجزيل لاهتمامه الكبير وعنايته الشديدة اللذين لازماه خلال اجرائه للعملية الجراحية للزميل السقباني التي تكللت بالنجاح والشفاء التام بفضل من الله، متمنيا من المولى عز وجل أن يديم عليه الصحة والعافية ويحقق له المزيد من النجاح والازدهار.

Patients from Jordan and Qatar appreciating my
service in the National newspapers

71

CHAPTER 13

Finally, Back to UK Again in 2009

As my family could not join me in Qatar due to my children's educational commitments and my wife's permanent job, my 3 years contract ended and I moved back to the UK in 2009 to start a two-month locum consultant neurosurgery post in Birmingham University Hospital, which was extended for nearly five years.

My consultant colleagues and the nursing staff in Birmingham were very kind and supportive, and I am indebted in particular to my sincere colleague, the clinical service lead of the unit, Mr Graham Flint, who was exceptionally considerate and empathetic.

In 2012, during the last two years of my service in Birmingham, I dedicated my work to spinal surgery only because all consultants were divided into two teams, cranial and spinal.

I officially retired from operative neurosurgery in 2014 with positive comments from many of the patients I treated and the uplifting Hospital Episodes Statistics (HES) data published by the trust. I finally settled into doing teaching and clinical activities overseas, as well as medicolegal work in the UK, which I started in 1998 when I worked at the Royal Free Hospital, having learnt many tips from my senior colleague, Mr Robert Maurice Williams, to whom I am indebted.

AS A VISITING CONSULTANT TO BASRAH NEUROSURGICAL UNIT

Having worked as consultant neurosurgeon, lecturer, and then assistant professor in Basrah for twelve years (1980–1992), I continued to feel that I owed the city and the university the obligation of delivering the further experience I gained since I had left in 1992. Therefore in 2003, I started repeated visits to the unit of one to two weeks up to three times per year to participate in the clinical and teaching activities, especially given that the majority of the current fifteen consultant neurosurgeons in the unit were my medical students and were very welcoming, and the unit was now well equipped with most modern radiological and operative facilities: CT and MRI scans, Gamma Knife, operating microscope, and more. I have always been privileged and praised during these visits.

THE OPERATIVE SPINAL CORD INJURY CASE

An unforgettable operative complication of injuring the spinal cord which every spinal surgeon always dreads to happen in the anterior cervical discectomy, (the operation of removing the herniated and degenerate intervertebral disc in the neck from the front), even after more than the one thousand cases I have done. It happened while I was assisting the registrar in a patient with advanced degenerative cervical spine, causing severe radiological and clinical anterior spinal cord compression. The spinal cord became banana shaped from the severe central cord compression. Whilst drilling the hard disc towards one side, it injured the cord and not the nerve root, and it only appeared first as a CSF leak. It taught me and my colleagues, when we discussed it in our weekly morbidity and mortality meeting, the expected hard lesson that no matter how experienced the surgeon may be, he or she can still encounter a very rare and serious surgical complication.

The two lessons to be learnt from this case were that very often it takes more courage to resist the temptation to operate than not to operate, and that when selecting patients for the operation, neurosurgeons in general should avoid wishful thinking and high expectations, particularly when operating on cases with advanced or long-standing neurological deficit, because the chance of reversing or even improving the deficit is very slim or even non-existent. This case reminded me also of the of few "millimetres difference between life and death" in such cases, which I learnt from Robin Illingworth during the early years of my training.

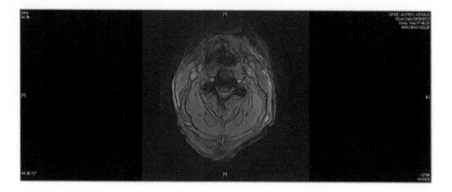

THE CHALLENGING CLINICAL NEGLIGENCE CLAIMS

With my two and a half decades of neurosurgical experience, I was happy to accept instructions to report on clinical negligence claims from the year 2000. I found that the majority had little chance of success because they were basically wishful thinking of the claimant or their families, particularly in cases of death.

One such case was a man in his fifties who died from a recurrent subarachnoid haemorrhage on the third day of his arrival to the neurosurgical unit. The neuroradiologist who was meant to coil his aneurysm was busy with another case, but another operating theatre was free for the available vascular surgeon to clip his aneurysm. After many discussions with the barrister and a joint telephone conference with two other experts, I lost the argument that he could have been saved if the vascular surgeon had clipped his aneurysm and pushed himself the extra mile. The barrister admitted that I lost the argument fifty-one to forty-nine and didn't want to proceed with the claim and go to court. This case represents what I came to believe: that the enthusiastic young consultant surgeons (in all surgical specialities) are keener to operate in the early years of their career, but their keenness fades away slowly with time towards the non-surgical means of management as they become more senior.

THE HAPPY MEMORIES FROM MY PATIENT'S FEEDBACK AND THE TRUST ASSESSMENT OF MY WORK

This is what matters in the end. I left it as a final reminder in the last few pages of this book, and though I still keep and treasure the thirteen thank-you cards from the many grateful patients I operated upon during my five years of service in Birmingham, I had complaints from only two patients who were not satisfied with my management during those years.

I acknowledge that no one is perfect, and like all surgeons, I also had my own problems and complications during the thirty-seven years of my active neurosurgical service in four countries.

However, I was finally very happy to end up with the uplifting and very positive objective evidence of the independent HES data published by the Birmingham Queen Elizabeth Trust when assessing my performance against my other twelve consultant neurosurgery colleagues in the unit during the last year of my service as a consultant neurosurgeon.

The HES (Hospital Episode Statistics) data is administrative and clinical data on operations and diagnosis collected from providers of NHS-funded hospital care used to analyse hospital activity for monitoring and improving the management of health and care services.

Before I left Birmingham and retired from clinical services, I was very pleased by the following comments I received in the last few months from two patients I operated upon. One was from the consultant ophthalmic surgeon, Andrew Jacks, who wrote to me twice stating:

"Ameen Staples out today. Wound healed well. Back and leg feel great. Thank you so much, you have been brilliant. I can lie flat for the first time in twenty years! Thank you".

He wrote to me again seven years later in September 2020 stating:

"Your surgery was magic and really helped. I recovered quickly and did lots of rehab exercises. I am fit and functional thanks to you".

The second feedback I received was from Ms Lynda Regan, who was denied spinal surgery for five years by another spinal surgical hospital. She was very happy and impressed by the outcome when she went home the next day after the minimally invasive spinal fusion operation I did for her. She was like a lifelong souvenir that neurosurgery is a gratifying, fascinating, and rewarding job:

"Hi Mr Ameen, just thought I would give you an update on my progress. I continue to feel better all of the time. No back pain at all, just an occasional ache. This is only when I have been on my feet all day and night. My energy levels amaze me, but it's a good job as two of my daughters in law are expecting babies very soon. And both are having health issues, so I am needed after work most days and weekends to help out with my grandchildren. Before my operation, this would not have been possible. I really enjoy being able to do so much with my grandchildren. I can walk anywhere and for long periods without any discomfort, and even now I don't take that long period for granted. I never believed that I would be able to walk without being in agony. I am totally happy with my life, whereas before my operation I wasn't at all sure how much longer I could go on. Each day just got more of a struggle than the day before. I was in such physical pain and emotionally drained just trying to get through the day. Now, when I'm tired, I'm also satisfied that I've been helpful to my family, and no longer do I have to say no when my grandchildren want me to do activities with them. My nine-year-old grandson is thrilled to bits with his new nanny. I knew he was worried about me before my operation; he kept asking how I was and telling me his mum wouldn't let him come too often, because his mum would say, "Nanny's not well." Now he accepts that I am the nanny he had five years ago. Without you taking a chance and giving me that operation, I would not be the person I am now. I will be eternally grateful".

Seven years later, she wrote to me again in September 2020:

"Lovely to hear from you, Mr Ameen Ameen. We are all well and trust you are too. I currently have no back problems related to my original back problem, and for that I will be forever in your debt.

Meeting you that day at the first hospital appointment changed my life. You listened, you reassured me, and you offered me the operation that gave me back the quality of life I had all but given up on. I spent five painful years with fruitless hospital visits in the care of another surgeon.

I think of you often. The day you retired, the medical profession lost not only a wonderful, talented surgeon but a true, caring gentleman, and I'm so glad you came into my life when you did. I enjoy my life free of crippling pain because of you.

I look forward to your book going on sale and wish you all the very best on the success of that book".

Great Mosque & Malwiya Tower in Samarra, completed 851 as the largest mosque in the world, destroyed by Halagu 1278, listed as world heritage site 2007

AL Kadhimiya Mosque Holly City by Twelver Shiites

Ingram Content Group UK Ltd.
Milton Keynes UK
UKHW040801240323
419106UK00001B/92